Granny Squares

...

Nanny Squares

NEW TWISTS FOR CLASSIC CROCHET

The Vanessa-Ann Collection

The Vanessa-Ann Collection Staff

Jo Packham and
Terrece Beesley Woodruff, owners
Kathi Allred
Gloria Baur
Trice Boerens
Vicki Burke
Kristen Jarchow
Susan Jorgensen
Margaret Marti
Barbara Milburn
Pamela Randall
Julie Truman
Nancy Whitley

Designers

Carrie Allen
Marlene Lund
Jo Packham
Pamela Roundy

Granny Squares ... Nanny Squares

NEW TWISTS FOR CLASSIC CROCHET

Oxmoor House®

Martha,
True and unconditional friendship is the rarest
and most valuable gift of all—and yet you give it so
unselfishly, so many times, in so many ways.

Thank you for everything but, most of all, thank you
for just being you.

Your friend,
Jo

© 1989 by Oxmoor House, Inc.
Book Division of Southern Progress Corporation
P.O. Box 832463, Birmingham, AL 35201

Library of Congress Catalog Number: 89-61579
ISBN: 0-8487-0769-9
Manufactured in the United States of America
First Printing 1989

Executive Editor: Nancy Janice Fitzpatrick
Production Manager: Jerry Higdon
Associate Production Manager: Rick Litton
Art Director: Bob Nance

Granny Squares, Nanny Squares

Editor: Margaret Allen Northen
Editorial Assistant: Susan Smith Cheatham
Production Assistant: Theresa L. Beste
Copy Chief: Mary Jean Haddin
Designer: Diana Smith Morrison
Artists: Barbara Ball, Eleanor Cameron
Photographers: Colleen Duffley, Ryne Hazen

The photographs in this book were taken at the homes of
Susan and Boyd Bingham, Ogden, Utah; Nan and Arnie
Smith, Ogden, Utah; and Edie and Courtney Stockstill, Salt
Lake City, Utah; as well as at Trends and Traditions, Ogden,
Utah; Ivywood, Ogden, Utah; Washington School Inn, Park
City, Utah; and Brigham Street Inn, Salt Lake City, Utah.
The Vanessa-Ann Collection very much appreciates the trust
and cooperation of each.

To find out how you can order *Cooking Light* magazine, write
to *Cooking Light*®, P.O. Box C-549, Birmingham, AL 35283.

Contents

■ ■ ■

Dear Friends:

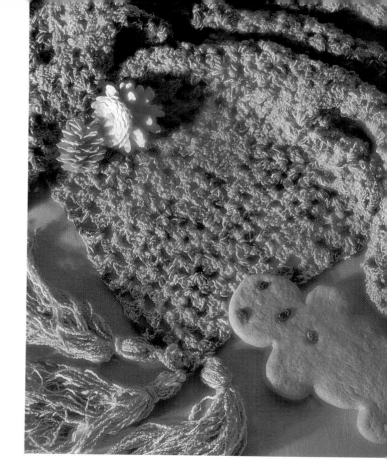

Autumn is my favorite time of year. It is a time to enjoy every idle hour, a time to begin something new or to gather golden moments and take a sentimental journey. One Sunday afternoon, with a fire in my fireplace and fall in the air, I put down my new album of crocheted designs that I had been working so hard on and I got out my old family albums. There were pictures of all of us doing nothing and everything—Mom and Daddy when they were much younger, Judy and me as children, and Grandma and Grandpa.

Grandma was my favorite. She had a quiet beauty that I will never forget. Whenever I think about her, there are a hundred memories that make me smile. She was wonderful, and she made such beautiful things. Every weekend, beginning in the fall and stretching through winter, I would walk into her living room and she would be sitting in that enormous green rocker crocheting. Everything she made was just like her: bright with color, alive with pattern, and full of love.

Grandma spent endless hours teaching me how to do what she so loved, and I know how proud and surprised she would be if she could see what I've done. I took her love of granny squares, her crocheting skills, and her wonderful sense of design and color, and I crocheted not only her old and cherished granny squares, but my own new and original "nanny squares"!

I wish Grandma could see my new album of crochet designs. She would enjoy looking through it as much as I enjoy the old family albums. She would see an afghan of traditional squares made with untraditional yarns whose colors recall the sounds of autumn and the taste of warm gingerbread. She'd see a flowery table cover crocheted in large and lacy nanny squares, perfect for a moment of quiet thought and jasmine-scented tea served in fragile china cups.

My daughter Sara's favorite is an afghan that is crocheted white-on-white and is as delicate and splendid as the first winter frost. It looks just like the one "Grandma-Great" gave her when she was born.

My son Justin's favorite is a simple adaptation of a nine-patch quilt square — this time in soft country colors. He loves to share it with his "other Grandma" when she reads to him on cold and snowy winter afternoons.

There is one my Mom particularly loves. It is made with the richest of yarns in shades of salmon and gray with just a touch of gold that sparkles in the light, and it is a perfect gift for the holiday season.

Grandma had the eye of a painter and the soul of a poet and a lasting love affair with handmade things. Her favorite afghan, always neatly folded at the foot of her bed, had a spirit of romance and was as sweet as a child's tender dream. Later I crocheted it from memory in colors that sang to me of spring. There is lavender intertwined with pink and the lightest blue touched with a whisper of the softest gray and, as I crocheted each square, it brought back treasured memories.

The baby afghans pictured in my new album are now wrapped neatly and tucked away in my cedar chest until my own grandchildren come to visit. Perhaps they, too, will come to appreciate Grandma's love of color and texture.

My album of crocheted *Granny Squares, Nanny Squares* is almost full. Besides the pieces mentioned here, there are many, many more. There are pillows in shapes and sizes to complement any decor, and luxurious linens for the kitchen, bedroom, and bath that stitch up quickly and are perfect gifts for the special people in your life. There's even a chapter full of fun-to-make Christmas items. I also included a chapter of squares to inspire the designer in you.

The old family albums and the crocheted pieces pictured in my new album bring back special feelings and memories. Now, curl up in your favorite chair with a supply of colorful yarns nearby and add a few pages to your own memory album.

Jo

General Directions
■ ■ ■

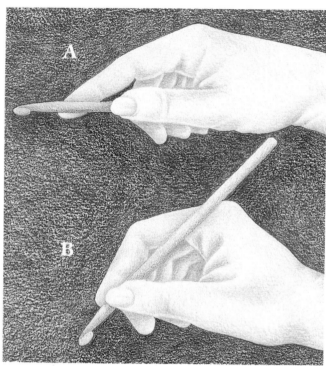

GAUGE

Before beginning a project, work a gauge swatch using the recommended-size hook. Measure an inch or two inches (as given in the gauge note); count and compare the number of stitches in the swatch with the designer's gauge. If you have fewer stitches in your swatch, try a smaller hook; if you have more stitches, try a larger hook.

CROCHET ABBREVIATIONS

beg	begin(ning)
bet	between
bk lp(s)	back loop(s)
ch	chain
ch-	refers to chain previously made
cont	continu(e) (ing)
dc	double crochet
dec	decrease(s) (d) (ing)
dtr	double triple crochet
ft lp(s)	front loop(s)
hdc	half double crochet
inc	increase(s) (d) (ing)
lp(s)	loop(s)
patt(s)	pattern(s)
prev	previous
qdtr	quadruple triple crochet
rem	remain(s) (ing)
rep	repeat
rnd(s)	round(s)
sc	single crochet
sk	skip
sl st	slip stitch
sp(s)	space(s)
st(s)	stitch(es)
tch	turning chain
tog	together
tr	triple crochet
yo	yarn over

Repeat whatever follows * as many times as indicated. "Rep from * 3 times more" means to work the directions a total of 4 times.

Work directions in parentheses and brackets the number of times or in the place specified.

Holding the Hook

Hold the hook as you would a piece of chalk (**A**) or a pencil (**B**). If your hook has a finger rest, position your thumb and opposing finger there for extra control.

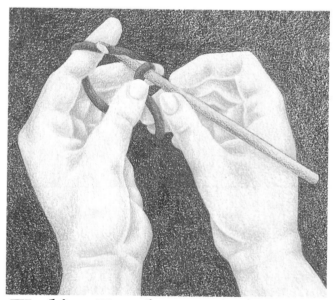

Working Together

Weave the yarn through the fingers of your left hand to control the amount of yarn fed into the work and to provide tension. Once work has begun, the thumb and middle finger of the left hand come into play, pressing together to hold the stitches just made.

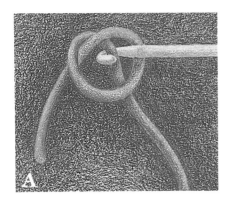

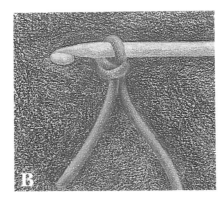

Slip Knot Diagram
Loop the yarn around and let the loose end of the yarn fall behind the loop to form a pretzel shape as shown. Insert the hook **(A)** and pull both ends of yarn to close the knot **(B)**. Careful—not too tight!

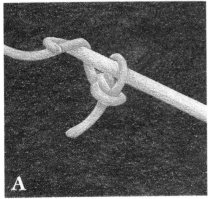

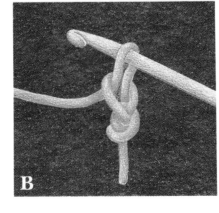

Chain Stitch Diagram
A. Place a slip knot on your hook. With hands in the position shown above, and with the thumb and middle finger of the left hand holding the yarn end, wrap the yarn up and over the hook (from back to front). This movement is called "yarn over (yo)" and is basic to every crochet stitch.

B. Use the hook to pull the yarn through the loop (lp) already on the hook. The combination of yo and pulling the yarn through the lp makes one chain stitch (ch).

C. Repeat until ch is desired length. Try to keep movements even and all the ch stitches (sts) the same size. Hold the ch near the working area to keep it from twisting. Count sts as shown in diagram. (Do not count lp on hook or slip knot.)

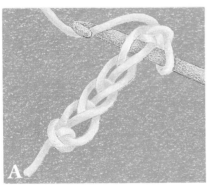

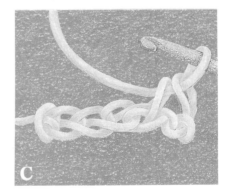

Single Crochet Diagram
A. Insert hook under top 2 lps of 2nd ch from hook and yo. (Always work sts through 2 lps unless instructions specify otherwise.)

B. Yo and pull yarn through ch (2 lps on hook).

C. Yo and pull yarn through 2 lps on hook (1 sc completed).

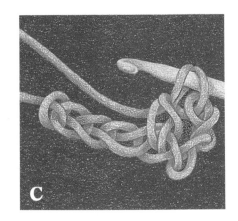

Double Crochet Diagram

A. Yo, insert hook into 3rd ch from hook and yo.

B. Pull yarn through ch (3 lps on hook).

C. Yo and pull yarn through 2 lps on hook (2 lps remaining).

D. Yo and pull yarn through 2 remaining (rem) lps on hook (1 dc completed).

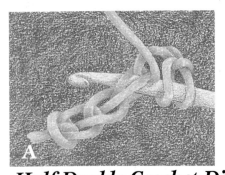

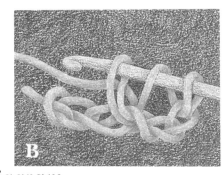

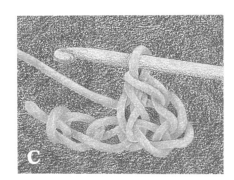

Half Double Crochet Diagram

A. Yo, insert hook into 2nd ch from hook.

B. Yo and pull yarn through ch (3 lps on hook).

C. Yo and pull yarn through all 3 lps on hook (1 hdc completed).

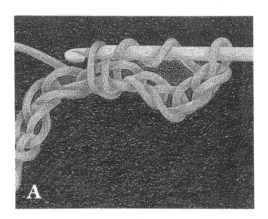

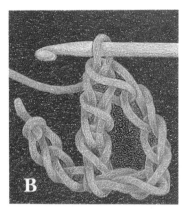

Triple Crochet Diagram

A. Yo twice, insert hook into 4th ch from hook. Yo and pull yarn through ch (4 lps on hook).

B. (Yo, pull through 2 lps on hook) 3 times (1 tr completed).

Slip Stitch Diagram

Here a slip stitch (sl st) is used to join a ring. Taking care not to twist ch, insert hook into first ch, yo, and pull yarn through ch and lp on hook (sl st completed).

To work sts in the ring, insert hook in center of ring and work around the base ch. Do not turn work when working in the round (rnd) unless specifically told to do so to achieve a special effect.

The sl st can also be used to join finished squares or to move across a group of sts without adding height to the work.

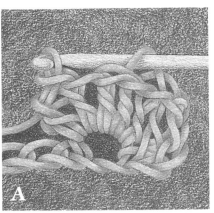

Working a Popcorn Stitch

A. Work specified number of sts in same st, draw up a lp in last st of group and drop lp from hook, insert hook in first st of group, and pick up dropped lp.
B. Draw yarn through and tighten, ch 1 to close popcorn.

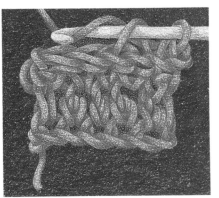

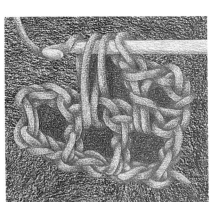

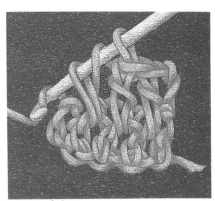

Working in Back Loop Only

Working into a Chain Space

Working Between Stitches

Working Around the Post

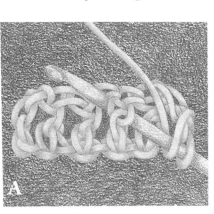

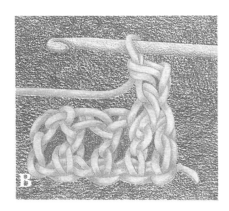

Elegant Afghans

...

CHAPTER ONE

Ivy League Afghan

Choose deep rich colors or soft pastels and work them as desired to stitch these squares of diagonal stripes.

■ ■ ■

FINISHED SIZE
Approximately 40″ x 60″.

MATERIALS
Bulky-weight wool: 45 oz. multicolor aqua and red (A); 22 oz. each green, red, blue; 28 oz. multicolor navy and red.

Size K crochet hook, or size to obtain gauge.

GAUGE
Square = 6½″.

DIRECTIONS
Note: Use yarn colors in different sequence for each square (see photograph). To change colors, do not ch 1 at the end of the row. Turn work, join new color, ch 1, and work the row according to the directions.

Square (make 54): Ch 2.

Row 1: Work 3 sc in 2nd ch from hook. Ch 1, turn.

Row 2: Work 2 sc in first sc, sc in next sc, 2 sc in last sc—5 sts. Ch 1, turn.

Row 3: Work 2 sc in first sc, sc in each of next 3 sc, 2 sc in last sc—7 sts. Ch 1, turn.

Row 4: Work 2 sc in first sc, sc evenly to last sc, work 2 sc in last sc. Ch 1, turn.

Rows 5-11: Rep row 4. After row 11—23 sts across.

Row 12: Draw up a lp in each of first 2 sts, yo and through all 3 lps on hook (1 sc dec completed), sc evenly to last 2 sts, dec 1 sc. Ch 1, turn.

Rep row 12 until only 3 sc rem.

Last row: Draw up a lp in each of last 3 sc, yo and through all lps on hook. Fasten off.

Border: Rnd 1: Join A with sl st in any corner, * 3 sc in corner, sc evenly to next corner, rep from * around, sl st to first sc.

Rnds 2 and 3: Sl st to center st of corner, rep rnd 1. Fasten off after rnd 3.

Assembly: Afghan is 6 squares wide and 9 squares long. Whipstitch squares tog. Be sure all diagonal stripes run in the same direction.

Border: Rnd 1: Join A with sl st in any corner, * 3 sc in corner, sc evenly to next corner, rep from * around, sl st to first sc.

Rnd 2: Sl st to center sc of corner, rep rnd 1. Fasten off.

Evening News

Different shades and textures of gray yarn worked in a variety of stitch patterns make a masculine afghan for cozy reading on crisp autumn evenings.

■ ■ ■

FINISHED SIZE
Approximately 47" x 70".

MATERIALS
Worsted-weight cotton-wool blend: 16 oz. medium gray (A).
Worsted-weight mohair blend: 11 oz. light gray (B).
Sportweight alpaca: 28 oz. dark gray (C).
Sportweight washable wool: 11 oz. medium gray (D).
Sportweight wool: 18 oz. dark gray (E); 14 oz. pearl gray (F).
Worsted-weight wool blend: 4 oz. gray (G).
Size E crochet hook, or size to obtain gauge.

GAUGE
Square = 7½".

DIRECTIONS
Note: Use patt sts and yarns as desired to make 54 (7½") squares. Work a border of sc sts on all squares before beg assembly. Be sure all squares are the same size. Listed below are some suggested st patts and hints on working with color and texture, as well as directions for a sample square. Another good source of design ideas is a stitch dictionary.

Texture hints: Sts can be worked in the front or back lps only to create ridges, or work in both front and back lps of each st for a bumpy texture. Working around the front or back post of a st in the row below gives a relief texture to the piece.

Color hints: Working a dc, tr, or dtr with light yarn around the front post of a st worked in a dark yarn will enhance the effect of a relief pattern. Use light and dark yarns alternately to create waves of shell sts or ripples of chevron sts.

Bobble: Keeping last lp of each st on hook, work desired number of sts in next st, yo and through all lps on hook to complete st.

Chained lp st: Do not beg a square with this st.
  Row 1: (Ch 6, sk 1 st, sc in next st) across, turn.
  Row 2: Ch 4, (sc in ch-6 lp, ch 1) across, end with dc in first ch of prev row.

Chevron st: Multiple of 10 + 1 (add 2 for base).
  Row 1: Sk 2 ch, dc in next ch, * dc in each of next 3 ch, 3-dc cluster over next 3 ch, dc in each of next 3 ch, 3 dc in next ch, rep from * across, end with 2 dc in last ch, turn.
  Row 2: Ch 3, dc in first st, * dc in each of next 3 sts, 3-dc cluster over next 3 sts, dc in each of next 3 sts, 3 dc in next st, rep from * across, end with 2 dc in top of tch, turn.
  Rep row 2 for patt.

Cluster: Keeping last lp of each st on hook, work 1 st in each of next desired number of sts, yo and through all lps on hook to complete st, ch 1.

Cross dc st: Multiple of 2 (add 2 for base).
  Ch 3, * sk 1 st, dc in next st, dc in sk st, rep from * across, end with dc in last st.

Crosshatch: Multiple of 7 + 4 (add 3 for base).
  Row 1: Sk 2 ch, 2 dc in next ch, * sk 3 ch, sc in next ch, ch 3, dc in each of next 3 ch, rep from * to last 4 ch, sk 3 ch, sc in last ch, turn.
  Row 2: Ch 3 for first dc, 2 dc in first sc, * sk 3 dc, sc in first st of ch-3, ch 3, dc in each of next 2 sts of ch-3, rep from * across, end with sk 2 dc, sc in top of tch, turn.
  Rep row 2 for patt.

Diagonal spike st: Multiple of 4 + 2 (add 2 for base).
  Row 1: Sk 3 ch, * dc in each of next 3 ch, sk next ch, yo, insert hook in same ch as first dc of prev 3-dc group, yo, draw up a lp loosely, complete st as a dc (spike st made), rep from * across, end with dc in last ch, turn.
  Row 2: Ch 3 for first dc, sk 1 st, dc in each of next 3 sts, sk next st, spike st in next st, rep from * across, end with dc in top of tch, turn.
  Rep row 2 for patt.

Fantail st: Multiple of 10 + 1 (add 1 for base).
  Row 1 (right side): Sc in 2nd ch from hook, sc in next ch, * sk 3 ch, (3 dc, ch 1, 3 dc) in next ch (fan completed), sk 3 ch, sc in next ch, ch 1, sk 1 ch, sc in next ch, rep from * across, end with sc in last ch, turn.
  Row 2 (wrong side): Ch 2 for first hdc, hdc in first st, * ch 3, sc in sp at center of next fan, ch 3, (hdc, ch 1, hdc) in next sp, rep from * across, end with 2 hdc in last sc, sk tch, turn.
  Row 3: Ch 3 for first dc, 3 dc in first st, * sc in next ch-3 sp, ch 1, sc in next ch-3 sp, fan in next ch-1 sp, rep from * across, end with 4 dc in tch, turn.
  Row 4: Ch 1, sc in first st, * ch 3, (hdc, ch 1, hdc) in next sp, ch 3, sc in sp at center of next fan, rep from * across, end with sc in tch, turn.
  Row 5: Ch 1, sc in first st, * sc in next ch-3 sp, fan in next ch-1 sp, sc in next ch-3 sp, ch 1, rep from * across, end with sc in last sc, sk tch, turn.
  Rep rows 2-5 for patt.

Knot st: Do not beg a square with this st.
  Row 1: Ch 1, sc in same st, * (pull up a ¾" lp, yo and through lp on hook, insert hook under single back strand, yo and draw through, yo and through both lps on hook) twice, sk 2 sts, sc in next st, rep from * across, turn.
  Row 2: Ch 5 for first dc and ch 2, sc in center knot of first lp, (ch 2, sc in center knot of next lp) across, end with ch 2, dc in beg ch of prev row.
  Rep rows 1 and 2 for patt.

Popcorn st: Work desired number of sts in next st, draw up a lp in last st of group and drop lp from hook, insert hook in first st of group, pick up dropped lp, draw through and tighten.

Puff st: Keeping all lps on hook, yo, insert hook in next st, pull up a lp, (yo, insert hook in same st, pull up a lp) 3 times, yo and through all 9 lps on hook.

Shell st: Multiple of 6 + 1 (add 1 for base).

Row 1: Sc in 2nd ch from hook, * sk 2 ch, 5 dc in next ch, sk 2 ch, sc in next ch, rep from * across, turn.

Row 2: Ch 3 for first dc, 2 dc in first st, * sk 2 dc, sc in next dc, sk 2 dc, 5 dc in next sc, rep from * across, end with 3 dc in last sc, sk tch, turn.

Row 3: Ch 1, sc in first st, * sk 2 dc, 5 dc in next dc, sk 2 dc, sc in next dc, rep from * across, end with sc in tch, turn.

Rep rows 2 and 3 for patt.

V st: * Sk 1 st, (2 dc, ch 1, 2 dc) in next st, rep from * across.

Zigzag lozenge st: Multiple of 2 + 1 (add 2 for base).

Row 1 (wrong side): Ch 2 for first hdc, hdc in next st, * sk 1 st, (hdc, ch 1, hdc) in next st, rep from * to last 2 sts, sk 1 st, 2 hdc in last st, turn.

Row 2 (right side): Ch 3 for first dc, dc in first st, * ch 1, 3-dc cluster in next sp, rep from * to last sp, ch 1, 2-dc cluster in top of tch, turn.

Row 3: Ch 2 for first hdc, sk first st, * (hdc, ch 1, hdc) in next sp, rep from * across, end with hdc in top of tch, turn.

Row 4: Ch 3 for first dc, sk first st, * 3-dc cluster in next sp, ch 1, rep from * across, end with dc in top of tch, turn.

Row 5: Ch 2 for first hdc, hdc in first st, * (hdc, ch 1, hdc) in next sp, rep from * across, end with 2 hdc in top of tch, turn.

Rep rows 2-5 for patt.

Sample square: With E or F, ch 40.

Row 1: Sc in 2nd ch from hook, ch 1, sk 1 ch, sc in next ch, * ch 2, sk 2 ch, sc in next ch, rep from * across, turn.

Row 2: Ch 3 for first dc, dc in next sc, 3 dc in each sp across, end with dc in last sc and beg ch, turn. Fasten off.

Row 3: Join D, ch 3 for first dc, dc in each of next 2 sts, (ch 2, sk 1 st, dc in each of next 2 sts) across, end with dc in last st, turn. Fasten off.

Row 4: Join B, ch 2 for first hdc, sk 1 dc, * hdc bet next 2 dc, puff st in next sp, ch 1, rep from * across, end with hdc in last dc, turn. Fasten off.

Row 5: Join C, ch 3 for first dc, * dc in top of next puff st, puff st in next hdc, rep from * across, end with dc in next hdc, ch 2, dc in last st, turn. Fasten off.

Row 6: Join F, ch 3 for first dc, dc in each st across, turn. Fasten off.

Row 7: Join C, * diagonal spike st in next st, sk 1 st, rep from * across, end with dc in last dc, turn. Fasten off.

Row 8: Join F and rep row 7, end with dc in last st, turn. Fasten off.

Row 9: Join D and rep row 7, end with 2 dc in last st, turn. Fasten off.

Row 10: Join F and work zigzag lozenge st across. Fasten off.

Row 11: Join C and work zigzag lozenge st across. Fasten off.

Row 12: Join F and work zigzag lozenge st across. Fasten off.

Row 13: Join D and work diagonal spike st across. Fasten off.

Row 14: Join B and work (puff st, dc) across. Fasten off.

Row 15: Join E, ch 4 for first dc and ch 1, * sk 1 st, dc in next st, ch 1, rep from * across, end with dc in last st. Fasten off.

Row 16: Join D and work zigzag lozenge st across. Fasten off.

Row 17: Join E, ch 3 for first dc, (3 dc in next st, sk 2 sts) across, end with dc in last st.

Row 18: Ch 2 for first hdc, hdc in each st across. Fasten off.

Border: Join C or E with sl st in any corner, * 3 sc in corner, sc evenly to next corner, rep from * around, sl st to first sc. *Note:* Be sure to work the same number of sc sts around each square for easy assembly.

Assembly: Afghan is 6 squares wide and 9 squares long. Whipstitch squares tog through bk lps only.

Edging: Rnd 1: Join C or E with sl st in any corner, ch 1, * (sc, ch 2, sc) in corner, (sk 1 st, sc in next st, ch 1) to next corner, rep from * around, sl st to first sc.

Rnd 2: Sl st in next sp, ch 1, * (sc, ch 1, sc) in corner sp, (sc in next ch-1 sp, ch 1) to next corner, rep from * around, sl st to first sc.

Rnds 3 and 4: Rep rnd 2. Fasten off after rnd 4.

Bouquet of Primroses

Select a slubbed yarn to set off the simplicity of this square.

■ ■ ■

FINISHED SIZE
Approximately 36″ x 43″.

MATERIALS
Sportweight silk: 34 oz. mauve; 27 oz. rose.
Size E crochet hook, or size to obtain gauge.

GAUGE
Square = 3½″.

DIRECTIONS
Square A: With mauve, ch 6, join with a sl st to form a ring.

Rnd 1: Ch 4 for first dc and ch 1, (dc in ring, ch 1) 11 times, sl st to 3rd ch of beg ch—12 dc counting beg ch. Fasten off.

Rnd 2: Join rose in any sp, ch 3 for first dc, keeping last lp of each st on hook, work 2 dc in same sp, yo and through all lps on hook (beg cluster completed), * ch 3, keeping last lp of each st on hook, work 3 dc in next sp, yo and through all lps on hook (cluster completed), rep from * 10 times more, end with ch 3, sl st to top of first cluster. Fasten off.

Rnd 3: Join mauve in any ch-3 sp, ch 1, sc in same sp, * ch 5, sc in next ch-3 sp, rep from * around, sl st to first sc. Fasten off.

Rnd 4: Join rose in any sp, ch 3 for first dc, (4 dc, ch 3, 5 dc) in same sp, * ch 1, sc in next sp, ch 5, sc in next sp, ch 1 **, (5 dc, ch 3, 5 dc) in next sp for corner, rep from * around, end last rep at **, sl st to top of beg ch. Fasten off.

Rep rnds 1-4 to make 30 each of squares A-D, working colors as follows:

	Rnd 1	Rnd 2	Rnd 3	Rnd 4
Square A	mauve	rose	mauve	rose
Square B	rose	mauve	rose	mauve
Square C	mauve	rose	rose	mauve
Square D	rose	mauve	mauve	rose

Border and assembly: Arrange squares as shown in placement diagram.

First square: Join mauve in any corner, ch 3 for first dc, 4 dc in same sp, * ch 3, sk 2 dc, sc in next dc, ch 5, sc in next ch-5 sp, ch 5, sk 2 dc, sc in next dc, ch 3, 5 dc in corner, rep from * around, sl st to top of beg ch. Fasten off.

Second square: Join mauve in any corner, ch 3 for first dc, 2 dc in same corner, sl st in center dc of corner on first square, 2 dc in same corner of 2nd square, ch 3, sk 2 dc on 2nd square, sc in next dc, ch 2, sc in next ch-5 sp on first square, ch 2, sc in next ch-5 sp on 2nd square, ch 2, sc in next ch-5 sp on first square, ch 2, sk 2 dc on 2nd square, sc in next dc, ch 2, 3 dc in next corner of 2nd square, sl st in center dc of corner on first square, 2 dc in same corner of 2nd square, complete square same as first square. Fasten off.

Join rem squares as established.

Border: Join mauve with sl st in any corner, ch 3 for first dc, 4 dc in same corner, * [ch 2, 3 dc in next sp (ch 1, 5 dc in next sp) twice, ch 1, 3 dc in next sp, ch 2, dc in corner st of square, dc in joining of squares, dc in corner st of next square] to next corner of afghan, work 5 dc in corner, rep from * around, sl st to top of beg ch.

A	B	C	D	A	B	C	D	A	B
D	A	B	C	D	A	B	C	D	A
C	D	A	B	C	D	A	B	C	D
B	C	D	A	B	C	D	A	B	C
A	B	C	D	A	B	C	D	A	B
D	A	B	C	D	A	B	C	D	A
C	D	A	B	C	D	A	B	C	D
B	C	D	A	B	C	D	A	B	C
A	B	C	D	A	B	C	D	A	B
D	A	B	C	D	A	B	C	D	A
C	D	A	B	C	D	A	B	C	D
B	C	D	A	B	C	D	A	B	C

Placement Diagram

Field of Pansies

For a throw as fresh as a spring-time garden, stud a delicate background of green with yellow and purple pansies.

■ ■ ■

FINISHED SIZE
Approximately 33" x 44".

MATERIALS
Size 5 pearl cotton thread: 75 (28-yd.) skeins green; 5 (28-yd.) skeins each yellow, deep purple; 3 (28-yd.) skeins each medium purple, medium rust; 4 (55-yd.) balls rust.

Size #7 steel crochet hook, or size to obtain gauge.

GAUGE
Square = 5½".

DIRECTIONS

Pansy: With yellow, ch 6, join with a sl st to form a ring.

Rnd 1: Ch 3 for first dc, 2 dc in ring, (ch 8, 3 dc in ring) 4 times, ch 8, sl st to top of beg ch — 5 ch-8 lps around. Fasten off.

Rnd 2: Join next color in center st of any 3-dc group, sc in same st, * ch 2, (tr, ch 1) 11 times in next lp, tr in same lp, ch 2, sc in center st of next 3-dc group, rep from * once more, ** ch 2, (dc, ch 1) 10 times in next lp, dc in same lp, ch 2, sc in center st of next 3-dc group, rep from ** twice more, sl st to first sc. Fasten off.

Rnd 3: Join next color in same sc as sl st, ch 4, * sc in next sp, ch 3, rep from * around, sl st to first ch of beg ch. Fasten off.

Rep rnds 1-3 above to make 12 each of pansies A-D, working colors as follows:

	Rnd 1	Rnd 2	Rnd 3
Pansy A	yellow	deep purple	medium purple
Pansy B	yellow	rust	deep purple
Pansy C	yellow	rust	yellow
Pansy D	yellow	rust	medium rust

Square: Rnd 1: Join green to ring at center of pansy bet any 3-dc groups, sc in same sp, * ch 5, sc in ring bet next 3-dc groups, rep from * around, sl st to first sc.

Rnd 2: Sl st in next ch-5 sp, ch 4 for first dc and ch 1, (dc, ch 1) in same lp 3 times, * (dc, ch 1) in next lp 4 times, rep from * around, sl st to 3rd ch of beg ch.

Rnd 3: Sl st in next ch-1 sp, sc in same sp, * ch 5, sc in next sp, rep from * around, sl st to first sc.

Rnd 4: Sl st to center of next sp, sc in same sp, * ch 5, sk next sp, (4 tr, ch 3, 4 tr) in next lp for corner, ch 5, sk next sp, sc in next sp **, ch 5, sc in next sp, rep from * around, end last rep at **, ch 2, dc in first sc.

Rnd 5: Sc in lp just made, * ch 3, sc in next sp, ch 5, keeping last lp of each st on hook, tr in each of next 4 tr, yo and through all lps on hook (4-tr cluster completed), ch 5, sl st in top of cluster to make a picot, ch 5, sl st in next sp, ch 5, make a 2-tr cluster in same sp, picot, ch 5, sl st in same sp, ch 5, 4-tr cluster over next 4 tr, picot, ch 5, sc in next sp, ch 3, sc in next lp, rep from * around, sl st to first sc. Fasten off.

Rnd 6: Join green in center sc on any edge of square, ch 5 for first dtr, 4 dtr in same sp, * ch 5, sc in next picot, ch 5, (2-dc cluster, ch 5, 2-dc cluster) in next picot, ch 5, sc in next picot, ch 5, sk next sc, 5 dtr in next sc, rep from * around, sl st to top of beg ch.

Rnd 7: Ch 3 for first dc, dc in each of next 5 sts, * 3 dc in next sp, ch 5, dc in next sp, ch 5, (3 dc, ch 5, 3 dc) in next sp, ch 5, dc in next sp, ch 5, 3 dc in next sp **, dc in each of next 5 dtr, rep from * around, end last rep at **, sl st to top of beg ch.

Rnd 8: Ch 3 for first dc, dc in each of next 5 dc, * ch 5, dc in next sp, ch 5, 3 dc in next sp, dc in each of next 3 dc, (3 dc, ch 5, 3 dc) in next corner, dc in each of next 3 dc, 3 dc in next sp, ch 5, dc in next sp, ch 5, sk 2 dc **, dc in each of next 7 dc, rep from * around, end last rep at **, dc in next dc, sl st to top of beg ch.

Rnd 9 (joining rnd): **First square:** Sl st in next dc, ch 3 for first dc, 2-dc cluster over next 2 dc, * (ch 5, dc in next sp) twice, ch 5, sk 3 dc, dc in each of next 6 dc, (3 dc, ch 5, 3 dc) in corner, dc in each of next 6 dc, (ch 5, dc in next sp) twice, ch 5 **, sk 2 dc, 3-dc cluster over next 3 dc, rep from * around, end last rep at **, sl st to top of first 2-dc cluster. Fasten off.

Second square: Sl st in next dc, ch 3 for first dc, 2-dc cluster over next 2 dc, (ch 5, dc in next sp) twice, ch 5, sk 3 dc, dc in each of next 6 dc, 3 dc in corner of 2nd square, ch 2, sc in corresponding corner of first square, ch 2, 3 dc in same corner of 2nd square, dc in each of next 6 dc, * (ch 2, sc in corresponding lp of first square, ch 2, dc in next sp of 2nd square) twice, ch 2, sc in corresponding lp of first square, ch 2 **, sk 2 dc on 2nd square, work a 3-dc cluster over next 3 dc on 2nd square, rep from * to **, sk 3 dc on 2nd square, dc in each of next 6 dc on 2nd square, (3 dc, ch 2) in corner of 2nd square, sc in corresponding corner of first square, 3 dc in same corner of 2nd square, complete square same as first square. Fasten off.

Cont to make and join squares as established, arranging pansies as desired for an afghan 6 squares wide and 8 squares long.

Cascade of Roses

Large and small roses climb a trellis of chain stitches, reminding one of the beauty of a formal rose garden.

■ ■ ■

FINISHED SIZE
Approximately 35″ square.

MATERIALS
Size 10 crochet thread: 10 (250-yd.) balls ecru.
Size #7 steel crochet hook, or size to obtain gauge.

GAUGE
Square = 7″.

DIRECTIONS
Small flower (make 100): Ch 6, join with a sl st to form a ring.

Rnd 1: Sc in ring, (ch 3, sc in ring) 5 times, sl st to first sc.

Rnd 2: * (Sc, 3 dc, sc) in next ch-3 sp, rep from * 4 times more, sl st to first sc. Fasten off.

Square (make 25): Ch 6, join with a sl st to form a ring.

Rnd 1: Ch 5 for first dc and ch 2, (dc in ring, ch 2) 7 times, sl st to 3rd ch of beg ch—8 spokes.

Rnd 2: Work (sc, 5 dc, sc) in each ch-2 sp, sl st to first sc—8 petals.

Rnd 3: Holding petals to front of work, * ch 4, sc from back of work in next dc of rnd 1, rep from * around, sl st to base of beg ch.

Rnd 4: Work (sc, 7 dc, sc) in each ch-4 lp around, sl st to first sc.

Rnd 5: Holding petals to front of work, * ch 5, sc from back of work bet next 2 petals, rep from * around, sl st to base of beg ch.

Rnd 6: Work (sc, 9 dc, sc) in each ch-5 lp around, sl st to first sc.

Rnd 7: Holding petals to front of work, * ch 6, sc from back of work bet next 2 petals, rep from * around, sl st to base of beg ch.

Rnd 8: Work (sc, 11 dc, sc) in each ch-6 lp around, sl st to first sc.

Rnd 9: * Ch 12, sk 5 sts, sc in next st, ch 12, sk 6 sts, sc in st bet petals, rep from * around, ch 6, dtr in base of beg ch.

Rnd 10: Sc in lp just made, * ch 10, sc in next lp, rep from * around, ch 5, dtr in first sc.

Rnd 11: Sc in lp just made, * ch 9, sc in 2nd ch from hook, hdc in next ch, dc in each of next 4 ch, hdc in next ch, sc in last ch, sl st in first sc (leaf made), (ch 10, sc in next lp) twice, sl st bet 2 sc at base of a small flower, sc in same lp (small flower joined), (ch 10, sc in next lp) twice, rep from * around, ch 5, dtr in first sc.

Rnd 12: Sc in lp just made, * ch 10, sc in tip of leaf, (ch 10, sc in next lp) twice, ch 10, sc in center dc of 3rd petal of small flower, (ch 10, sc in next lp) twice, rep from * around, ch 5, dtr in first sc.

Rnd 13: Sc in lp just made, * ch 8, 5 sc in next lp, 3 sc in st at point of leaf, 5 sc in next lp, ch 8, sc in next lp, ch 8, (3 sc in next lp) twice, ch 8 **, sc in next lp, rep from * around, end last rep at **, ch 4, tr in first sc.

Rnd 14: Sc in lp just made, * ch 6, sc in next lp, ch 4, dc in each of next 2 sc, ch 3, sk 3 sts, dc in next sc, 3 dc in next sc for corner, dc in next sc, ch 3, sk 3 sts, dc in each of next 2 sc, ch 4, sc in next lp, ch 6, sc in next lp, ch 4, sc in next 6 sc, ch 4, sc in next lp, rep from * around, ch 2, dc in first sc.

Rnd 15 (joining rnd): **First square:** Sc in lp just made, (ch 7, sc in next lp) 3 times, ch 7, * sc in center st of corner, (ch 7, sc in next lp) 4 times, ch 7, rep from * around, sl st to first sc. Fasten off.

Second square: Sc in lp just made, (ch 7, sc in next lp) 3 times, ch 7, sc in center st of corner, (ch 3, sl st in corresponding lp of first square, ch 3, sc in next lp of 2nd square) 4 times, ch 3, sl st in next lp of first square, ch 3, sk 3 sc on 2nd square, sc in next sc, (ch 3, sl st in next lp of first square, ch 3, sc in next lp of 2nd square) 4 times, ch 3, sl st in next lp of first square, ch 3, sc in center st of corner on 2nd square, complete square same as first square. Fasten off.

Cont to make and join squares as established for a throw 5 squares wide and 5 squares long.

A Classic Coverlet

Raised petal flowers and popcorn stitches make a classic bedspread.

■ ■ ■

FINISHED SIZE
Approximately 62″ x 104″.

MATERIALS
Size 10 crochet thread: 53 (250-yd.) balls ecru.
Size #7 steel crochet hook, or size to obtain gauge.

GAUGE
Motif = 15″ diameter.

DIRECTIONS

Whole motif (make 38): Ch 9, join with a sl st to form a ring.

Rnd 1: Ch 1, 18 sc in ring, sl st to first sc.

Rnd 2: Ch 3 for first dc, work 4 dc in bk lp of next st, draw up a lp in last st of group and drop lp from hook, insert hook in top of beg ch-3, pick up dropped lp, draw through and tighten to close (beg popcorn st completed), ch 2, * sk 1 sc, work 5 dc in bk lp of next st, draw up a lp in last st of group and drop lp from hook, insert hook in first dc of group, pick up dropped lp, draw through and tighten to close (popcorn st completed), ch 2, rep from * around, sl st to top of beg popcorn.

Rnd 3: Sl st in next sp, ch 3 for first dc, work beg popcorn in same sp, ch 1, * (popcorn, ch 1, popcorn) in next sp, ch 1, rep from * around, end with popcorn in same sp as beg, ch 1, sl st to top of beg popcorn — 18 popcorns.

Rnd 4: Ch 5 for first dc and ch 2, * dc in top of next popcorn, ch 2, rep from * around, sl st to 3rd ch of beg ch.

Rnd 5: Ch 1, 3 sc in same st, * sc in next sp, 3 sc in next dc, rep from * around, sl st to first sc.

Rnds 6-17: Working in bk lps only, * 3 sc in next sc (center st of 3-sc group), sc in each st to center st of next 3-sc group, rep from * around, sl st to first sc. *Note:* Each 3-sc group is the beg of a petal — 18 petals.

Rnd 18: Mark the center st bet petals with a colored thread. Sl st in each sc to within 5 sts of first marker, * holding marker in left hand, fold next petal back to 5 sts from marker with right sides facing. Working through both thicknesses, work 1 sc in each of next 5 sts, ch 4, rep from * around, sl st to first sc.

Rnd 19: Working in bk lps only, sc in each of next 2 sc, * 3 sc in next sc for corner, sc in each of next 26 sts, rep from * around, end with sc in each of next 24 sts, sl st to first sc.

Rnds 20-24: Sc in each sc to corner, work 3 sc in center st of each 3-sc group for corner, sl st to first sc.

Rnd 25: Sl st to center st of next 3-sc group, ch 4 for first dc and ch 1, dc in same st, * (ch 1, sk 1 sc, dc in next sc) 18 times, ch 1, sk 1 st **, work (dc, ch 1, dc) in center st of next 3-sc group for corner, rep from * around, end last rep at **, sl st to 3rd ch of beg ch — 120 sps.

Rnd 26: Sl st in next sp, working in ft lps only, ch 4 for first dc and ch 1, dc in same sp, * (ch 1, sk 1 st, dc in next sp) 19 times, ch 1 **, work (dc, ch 1, dc) in next ch-1 sp for corner, rep from * around, end last rep at **, sl st to 3rd ch of beg ch — 126 sps.

Rnd 27: Work * 3 sc in sp, sc in each of next 41 sts, rep from * around, sl st to first sc — 264 sts.

Rnd 28: Sl st to center st of next 3-sc group, * 3 sc in same st, sc in each of next 3 sc, (popcorn in next sc, sc in each of next 5 sc) 6 times, popcorn in next sc, sc in each of next 3 sc, rep from * around, sl st to first sc.

Rnd 29: Sl st to center st of 3-sc group, * 3 sc in same st, sc in each st to center st of next 3-sc group, rep from * around, sl st to first sc.

Rnd 30: Sl st to center st of 3-sc group, * 3 sc in same st, sc in each of next 2 sc, (popcorn in next sc, sc in each of next 5 sc) 7 times, popcorn in next sc, sc in each of next 2 sc, rep from * around, sl st to first sc.

Rnd 31: Rep rnd 29.

Rnd 32: Sl st to center st of 3-sc group, ch 4 for first dc and ch 1, dc in same st, * (ch 1, sk 1 sc, dc in next sc) 25 times, ch 1, (dc, ch 1, dc) in center st of next 3-sc group for corner, rep from * around, sl st to 3rd ch of beg ch.

Rnd 33: Sl st in next sp, ch 4 for first dc and ch 1, dc in same sp, * (ch 1, dc in next sp) 26 times, ch 1, (dc, ch 1, dc) in next corner sp, rep from * around, sl st to 3rd ch of beg ch.

Rnd 34: Sl st in next sp, * 3 sc in sp, sc in each of next 55 sts, rep from * around, sl st to first sc.

Rnd 35: Sl st to center st of 3-sc group, * 3 sc in same st, sc in each of next 4 sc, (popcorn in next sc, sc in each of next 5 sc) 8 times, popcorn in next sc, sc in each of next 4 sc, rep from * around, sl st to first sc.

Rnd 36: Sl st to center st of 3-sc group, * 3 sc in same st, sc in each st to center st of next 3-sc group, rep from * around, sl st to first sc.

Rnd 37: Sl st to center st of 3-sc group, * 3 sc in same st, sc in each of next 3 sc, (popcorn in next sc, sc in each of next 5 sc) 9 times, popcorn in next sc, sc in each of next 3 sc, rep from * around, sl st to first sc.

Rnd 38: Rep rnd 36.

Rnd 39: Sl st to center st of 3-sc group, * 3 sc in same st, sc in each of next 2 sc, (popcorn in next sc, sc in each of next 5 sc) 10 times, popcorn in next sc, sc in each of next 2 sc, rep from * around, sl st to first sc.

Rnd 40: Rep rnd 36.

Rnd 41: Sl st to center st of 3-sc group, ch 4 for first dc and ch 1, dc in same st, * (ch 1, sk 1 sc, dc in next sc) 34 times, ch 1, sk 2 sts, (dc, ch 1, dc) in center st of next 3-sc group for corner, rep from * around, sl st to 3rd ch of beg ch.

Rnd 42: Sl st in next sp, ch 4 for first dc and ch 1, dc in same sp, * (ch 1, dc in next sp) 35 times, ch 1, (dc, ch 1, dc) in next sp for corner, rep from * around, sl st to first sc. Fasten off.

Half motif (make 4): Ch 9, join with a sl st to form a ring.

Row 1: Work 9 sc in ring, sl st in last 3 ch of ring, sl st to first sc.

Row 2: Ch 3 for first dc, work 4 dc in bk lp of next st, draw up a lp in last st of group and drop lp from hook, insert hook in top of beg ch-3, pick up dropped lp, draw through and tighten to close (beg popcorn completed), * ch 2, sk 1 sc, work 5 dc in bk lp of next st, draw up a lp in last st of group and drop lp from hook, insert hook in first dc of group, pick up dropped lp, draw through and tighten to close (popcorn st completed), rep from * 3 times more. Fasten off.

Row 3: Join thread in top of beg popcorn of prev row, ch 3 for first dc, work beg popcorn in same st, * ch 1, (popcorn, ch 1, popcorn) in next sp, rep from * across — 9 popcorns. Fasten off.

Row 4: Join thread in top of beg popcorn of prev row, ch 5 for first dc and ch 2, * dc in next sp, ch 2, dc in next popcorn, ch 2, rep from * across, omit ch 2 at end of last rep — 8 sps. Fasten off.

Row 5: Join thread in 3rd ch of beg ch-5 of prev row, * sc in next sp, 3 sc in next dc, rep from * across. Fasten off.

Rows 6-17: Join thread in first sc of prev row, working in bk lps only, sc in each of next 2 sts, * 3 sc in center st of 3-sc group, sc in each st to center st of next 3-sc group, rep from * across. Fasten off.

Row 18: Mark the center st bet petals with a colored thread. Place a pin in 9th sc from beg of prev row. With wrong side facing, join thread to sc marked by pin, ch 5, sk 3 sc, sc in each of next 5 sc, turn work so right side is facing, * ch 5, holding marker in left hand, fold next petal back to 5 sts from marker, working through both thicknesses, sc in each of next 5 sts, rep from * 6 times more, with wrong side of last petal facing, sc in each of last 5 sc — 85 sts. Fasten off.

Row 19: Join thread to first ch of beg ch-5 of prev row, working in bk lps only, sc evenly across row — 85 sts. Fasten off.

Row 20: Join thread in first sc of prev row, 2 sc in same st, (sc in each of next 27 sc, 3 sc in next sc) twice, sc in each of next 27 sc, 2 sc in last sc. Fasten off.

Rows 21-24: Join thread in first sc of prev row, 2 sc in same st, * sc in each sc to center st of 3-sc group, 3 sc in center st of 3-sc group, rep from * across, end with 2 sc in last sc. Fasten off.

Row 25: Join thread in first sc of prev row, ch 4 for first dc and ch 1, dc in same st, * (ch 1, sk 1 sc, dc in next sc) 18 times, ch 1, (dc, ch 1, dc) in center st of next 3-sc group, rep from * across, end with (dc, ch 1, dc) in last sc. Fasten off.

Rows 26-40: Rep rnds 26-40 of whole motif above. Remember to fasten off at the end of each row. Join thread in first st of prev row.

Rnd 41: Join thread in first sc of prev row, ch 4 for first dc and ch 1, dc in same st, * (ch 1, sk 1 sc, dc in next sc) 34 times, ch 1, (dc, ch 1, dc) in center st of next 3-sc group, rep from * across 3 edges, end with (dc, ch 1, dc) in last sc of 3rd edge of motif. Cont working along last edge of motif as follows: (Ch 1, sk 1 sc, dc in next sc) to beg corner, end with ch 1, sl st to 3rd ch of beg ch. Do not fasten off.

Rnd 42: Sl st in next sp, ch 4 for first dc and ch 1, dc in same sp, * (ch 1, dc in next sp) to corner, (dc, ch 1, dc) in corner, rep from * around, sl st to 3rd ch of beg ch. Fasten off.

Assembly: With right sides facing, whipstitch whole motifs tog in 3 rows of 8 and 2 rows of 7.

With right sides facing, whipstitch rows tog, alternating rows of 8 with rows of 7.

With right sides facing, whipstitch 2 half motifs in sps at top of coverlet. Rep to join rem 2 half motifs in sps at bottom of coverlet.

Edging: Join thread with sl st in top right-hand corner of coverlet. Ch 3 for first dc, dc in same sp, work * [(2 dc in each sp) 3 times, ch 5, sl st in 5th ch from hook to make a picot] to next corner, (2 dc, picot, 2 dc) in corner, rep from * around, sl st to top of beg ch. Fasten off.

Gingerbread Throw

Update the granny square by working with novelty yarns.

■ ■ ■

FINISHED SIZE
Approximately 42″ x 57″.

MATERIALS
Worsted-weight cotton blend novelty texture: 30 oz. multicolor brown, blue, and beige (A); 7 oz. multicolor beige, off-white, tan, and brown (B).

Fingering-weight cotton blend thick-and-thin texture: 11 oz. light brown (C).

Size E crochet hook, or size to obtain gauge.

GAUGE
Square = 5″.

DIRECTIONS
Square (make 88): With A, ch 6, join with a sl st to form a ring.

Rnd 1: Ch 3 for first dc, 2 dc in ring, (ch 3, 3 dc in ring) 3 times, ch 3, sl st to top of beg ch.

Rnd 2: Sl st in next ch-3 sp, ch 3 for first dc, work (2 dc, ch 3, 3 dc) in same sp, * ch 2, work (3 dc, ch 3, 3 dc) in corner, rep from * twice more, ch 2, sl st to top of beg ch.

Rnd 3: Sl st in next ch-3 sp, ch 3 for first dc, (2 dc, ch 3, 3 dc) in same sp for corner, * ch 2, 3 dc in next sp, ch 2, (3 dc, ch 3, 3 dc) in next corner, rep from * around, sl st to top of beg ch.

Rnd 4: Sl st in ch-3 sp, ch 3 for first dc, (2 dc, 3, 3 dc) in same corner, * (ch 2, 3 dc in next sp) twice, ch 2, (3 dc, ch 3, 3 dc) in next corner, rep from * around, sl st to top of beg ch. Fasten off.

Rnd 5: Join C in any corner, ch 3 for first dc, (2 dc, ch 3, 3 dc) in same corner, * (ch 2, 3 dc in next sp) 3 times, ch 2, (3 dc, ch 3, 3 dc) in next corner, rep from * around, sl st to top of beg ch. Fasten off.

Assembly: Afghan is 8 squares wide and 11 squares long. With wrong sides facing, sl st squares tog through bk lps only.

Border: Rnd 1: Join C in any corner, ch 3 for first dc, (2 dc, ch 3, 3 dc) in same corner sp, * (ch 2, 3 dc in next sp) to next corner, work (3 dc, ch 3, 3 dc) in corner, rep from * around, sl st to top of beg ch. Fasten off.

Rnd 2: Join A in any corner and rep rnd 1. Fasten off.

Tassels (make 12): For each tassel, cut 8 (14″) strands of A, 20 (14″) strands of B, and 6 (14″) strands of C. Gather all strands and fold in half. Tie a piece of yarn around strands at fold. Tie another piece of yarn tightly around strands about 1″ below fold. Attach a tassel to ch-3 sp in each corner and to ch-3 sps on either side of corner.

Soft Pinks

Smooth mercerized yarn worked in rows of clusters joins these floral motif squares.

■ ■ ■

FINISHED SIZE
Approximately 37″ x 52″.

MATERIALS
Worsted-weight mercerized cotton: 16 oz. beige; 18 oz. peach; 14 oz. green.
Size E crochet hook, or size to obtain gauge.

GAUGE
Square = 3½″.

DIRECTIONS
Square A: With beige, ch 6, join with a sl st to form a ring.

Rnd 1: Ch 5 for first dc and ch 2, (dc in ring, ch 2) 7 times, sl st to 3rd ch of beg ch. Fasten off.

Rnd 2: Join green in any sp, ch 3 for first dc, keeping last lp of each st on hook, work 3 dc in same sp, yo and through all lps on hook (beg cluster completed), ch 5, * keeping last lp of each st on hook, work 4 dc in next sp, yo and through all lps on hook (cluster completed), rep from * around, ch 5, sl st to top of first cluster. Fasten off.

Rnd 3: Join peach in top of any cluster, ch 1, sc in same st, * ch 2, working around ch-5 lp of rnd 2, dc in next dc of rnd 1, ch 2, sc in top of next cluster, rep from * around, sl st to first sc.

Rnd 4: Sl st in next sp, ch 1, sc in same sp, * ch 3, sc in next sp, rep from * around, sl st to first sc.

Rnd 5: Ch 3 for first dc, (dc, ch 2, 2 dc) in same sp, * ch 2, sc in next sp, (ch 3, sc in next sp) twice, ch 2, (2 dc, ch 2, 2 dc) in next sp for corner, rep from * around, sl st to first sc. Fasten off.

Rep rnds 1-5, to make a total of 69 squares, working colors as follows:

	Rnd 1	Rnd 2	Rnds 3-5
Square A (make 20)	beige	green	peach
Square B (make 20)	green	beige	peach
Square C (make 12)	green	peach	beige
Square D (make 12)	peach	green	beige
Square E (make 3)	beige	peach	green
Square F (make 2)	peach	beige	green

Assembly: Beg with square E, whipstitch squares E and F tog, alternately, in a row (see photograph).

Rnd 1: Join peach in any corner, work (beg cluster, ch 3, cluster) in same corner, * (cluster, ch 1) in each sp to next corner, (cluster, ch 3, cluster) in corner, rep from * around, sl st to top of beg cluster, sl st in next sp.

Rnds 2-8: Rep rnd 1. Fasten off after rnd 8.

Beg at corner with square C and beige, whipstitch squares C and D, alternately, to rnd 8 of afghan (see photograph).

Rnd 9: With peach, rep rnd 1 above. Fasten off.

Rnds 10-15: With green, rep rnd 1 above. Fasten off after rnd 15.

Rnd 16: With beige, rep rnd 1 above. Fasten off.

Beg at corner with square A and beige, whipstitch squares A and B, alternately, to rnd 16 of afghan (see photograph).

Border: Rnds 1 and 2: Join beige with sl st in any corner, (beg cluster, ch 3, cluster) in same corner, * (cluster, ch 1) in each sp to next corner, (cluster, ch 3, cluster) in corner, rep from * around, sl st to top of beg cluster, sl st in next sp.

Rnd 3: Work * (sc, hdc, 2 dc, hdc, sc) in next sp, sc in top of next cluster, sc in next sp, rep from * around, sl st to first sc. Fasten off.

Crocheted Sampler

These squares feature fun-to-make specialty stitches. Rotate yarn colors from square to square to achieve the sampler effect.

FINISHED SIZE
Afghan: Approximately 49″ square.
Pillow: Approximately 13″ square.

MATERIALS
Sportweight linen-acrylic blend: 11 oz. light green; 16 oz. beige.
Sportweight cotton thick-and-thin texture: 13 oz. each medium green, cream.
Worsted-weight cotton: 11 oz. apricot.
Bulky-weight mohair blend: 14 oz. pastel blend.
Size G crochet hook, or size to obtain gauge.
3 yards (45″-wide) cream fabric.
Thread to match.
6 yards (½″) cording.
2 (13″-square) pillow forms.

GAUGE
Square = 6½″.

DIRECTIONS
Note: To avoid holes when changing colors, bring up new color from under dropped color. Always bring up new color as last yo of old color. Do not carry yarn across row except where indicated.

Square A: With first color, ch 25.
Row 1: Sc in 2nd ch from hook and each ch across, turn.
Row 2: Ch 1, sc in ft lp only of each st across, turn.
Row 3 (fan st): With base color, ch 1, draw up a lp in each of next 3 sc, yo and through 1 lp on hook, (yo and through 2 lps on hook) 3 times (4 afghan sts made), draw up lp with fan color, drop and tighten base color, ch 4, sk first ch, draw up a lp loosely in each of rem 3 ch, insert hook from right to left around vertical bar of each afghan st, draw up a lp loosely in each of first 3 afghan sts—7 lps on hook, (leave last afghan st unworked), yo and through all 7 lps on hook (fan completed), ch 1 to tighten center of fan, * draw up lp with base color, drop and tighten fan color, draw up a lp in center of prev fan, draw up a lp in back of last lp of fan, draw up a lp in last unworked afghan st and in each of next 3 sc sts—7 lps on hook, yo and through 1 lp on hook, (yo and through 2 lps on hook) 6 times (7 afghan sts made), draw up a lp with fan color, drop base color and tighten, draw up a lp in each of first 6 afghan sts (leave last afghan st unworked), yo and through all 7 lps on hook, ch 1 to tighten center of fan, rep from * 6 times more, draw up a lp with base color, drop and tighten fan color, draw up a lp in center of prev fan, draw up a lp in back of last lp of fan, draw up a lp in last unworked afghan st and each of last 2 sts—6 lps on hook, yo and through 1 lp on hook, (yo and through 2 lps on hook) 5 times (6 afghan sts made), draw up a lp with fan color, drop and tighten base color, draw up a lp in each of last 6 afghan sts, yo and through all 7 lps on hook, ch 1, draw up a lp with base color, fasten off fan color, turn—9 fans across.
Row 4: Ch 1, sc in center of first fan, * sc in top lp of same fan, sc in top of next afghan st, sc in center of next fan, rep from * across, end with sc in top lp of last fan, sc in ch, turn—25 sts across.
Row 5: Ch 1, sc in each st across, turn.
Row 6: Ch 1, sc in ft lp only of each st across, turn. Fasten off.
Row 7: Join next color, ch 1, working in bk lps only, * sc in next st, ch 1, sk next st, rep from * across, turn. Fasten off.
Row 8: Join next color, ch 1, sc in ft lp only of each st across, turn. Fasten off.
Row 9: Join next color, ch 1, sc in bk lp only of each st across, turn. Fasten off.
Rows 10 and 11: Join next color, ch 1, sc in ft lp only of each st across, turn.
Row 12: Ch 1, sc in each of next 2 sts, * sc in ft lp only of next st, sc in each of next 3 sts, rep from * across, end with sc in each of last 2 sc, turn.
Row 13: Ch 1, sc in each of next 2 sts, * join next color, working in unworked lp of st on row 11 and keeping last lp of each st on hook, work 5 dc in same st, pick up prev color, yo and through all lps on hook (bobble completed), sc in each of next 3 sc, rep from * 4 times more, bobble in next st, sc in last st, turn—6 bobbles across.
Rows 14 and 15: Ch 1, sc in each st across, turn. Fasten off after row 15.

Row 16: Join next color, ch 1, sc in ft lp only of each st across, turn. Fasten off.

Row 17: Join next color, ch 1, sc in ft lp only of each st across, turn. Fasten off.

Row 18: Join next color, ch 1, sc in ft lp only of each st across, turn.

Row 19: Ch 1, sc in bk lp only of each st across, turn. Fasten off.

Row 20: Join next color, ch 1, sc in ft lp only of each st across, turn.

Rows 21 and 22: Ch 1, sc in each st across, turn.

Row 23: *Note:* Carry yarn not in use across this row by working over it with the next group of sts. Ch 1, sc in each of next 3 sts, * join next color with last yo of last sc, pull up a lp in same st as prev sc, pull up a lp in each of next 2 sts, pick up prev color, yo and through all lps on hook (dot made), sc in same st as last lp, sc in each of next 2 sts, rep from * 4 times more, sc in last sc, turn. Fasten off dot color.

Rows 24 and 25: Ch 1, sc in each st across, turn.

Row 26: Ch 1, sl st in ft lp only of each st across. Do not turn or fasten off.

Border: Row 1: With right side facing and working down side edge of square, ch 1, sc in each row to fan st row, (sk 1 st, sc in next st) twice, sc in each of last 2 rows, turn.

Row 2: Ch 1, sl st in ft lp only of each st across. Fasten off.

Rep rows 1 and 2 on rem side edge of square.

Square B: With first color, ch 4, join with a sl st to form a ring.

Rnd 1: Ch 1, 12 sc in ring, sl st to first sc.

Rnd 2: Ch 1, * 3 sc in same st for corner, sc in each of next 2 sts, rep from * 3 times more, sl st to first sc. Fasten off.

Rnd 3: Join next color in center st of any corner, ch 1, working in bk lps only, * 3 sc in same st for corner, sc evenly to next corner, rep from * around, sl st to first sc.

Rnd 4: Ch 1, * sc evenly to next corner, 3 sc in corner, rep from * around, sl st to first sc.

Rnd 5: Sl st to center st of corner 3-sc group, ch 1, * 3 sc in center st for corner, sc in next st, sc in bk lp only of next st, sc in each of next 4 sts, sc in bk lp only of next st, sc in next st, rep from * around, sl st to first sc.

Rnd 6: Sl st to center st of corner 3-sc group, ch 1, * 3 sc in center st for corner, sc in each of next 2 sts, join new color, working in ft lp of sc on rnd 4

and keeping last lp of each st on hook, work 3 dc in same st, pick up prev color, yo and through all lps on hook (bobble completed), ch 1, sc in each of next 4 sts, bobble in next st, sc in each of next 2 sts, rep from * around, sl st to first sc. Fasten off bobble color.

Rnd 7: Ch 1, * sc evenly to next corner, 3 sc in next st for corner, rep from * around, sl st to first sc. Fasten off.

Rnd 8: Join next color in center st of any corner, ch 3 for first dc, 2 dc in same st for corner, * (ch 1, sk 1 st, dc in next st) to next corner, 3 dc in corner, rep from * around, sl st to top of beg ch. Fasten off.

Rnd 9: Join next color in sp before center st of any corner, ch 3 for first dc, keeping last lp of each st on hook, work 3 dc in same sp, yo and through all lps on hook (beg cluster completed), ch 2 for corner, keeping last lp of each st on hook, work 4 dc in sp bet next 2 sts of corner, yo and through all lps on hook (cluster completed), * (ch 1, cluster in next ch-1 sp) to next corner, ch 1, cluster bet next 2 sts of corner, ch 2, cluster bet next 2 sts of corner, rep from * around, sl st to top of first cluster. Fasten off.

Rnd 10: Join next color in any corner sp, ch 1, * 3 sc in same sp for corner, sc evenly to next corner, rep from * around, sl st to first sc.

Rnd 11: Ch 1, working in bk lps only, * sc evenly to next corner, 3 sc in corner, rep from * around, sl st to first sc. Fasten off.

Afghan: Square A1 (make 4): Follow directions for square A and work colors as follows: Rows 1-6: Beige. On row 3, use beige for base color and pastel blend for fans. Row 7: Apricot. Row 8: Cream. Row 9: Light green. Rows 10-15: Beige. On row 13, work bobbles as follows: Apricot, cream, pastel blend, light green, cream, apricot. Row 16: Apricot. Row 17: Cream. Rows 18 and 19: Light green. Rows 20-26: Beige. On row 23, work dots with cream.

Square A2 (make 16): Follow directions for square A and work colors as follows: Rows 1-6: Light green or medium green. On row 3, use light green or medium green for base color and pastel blend for fans. Row 7: Cream. Row 8: Apricot. Row 9: Pastel blend. Rows 10-15: Light green or medium green. On row 13, work bobbles as follows: Apricot, cream, pastel blend, beige, cream, apricot. Row 16: Cream. Row 17: Apricot. Rows 18 and 19: Pastel blend. Rows 20-26: Light green or medium green. On row 23, work dots with cream. *Note:* Make several of these squares using colors at random on rows 7-19 and row 23 dots.

Square B1 (make 23): Follow directions for square B and work colors as follows: Rnds 1 and 2: Beige. Rnds 3-7: Light green or medium green. On rnd 6, work bobbles with cream. Rnd 8: Apricot. Rnd 9: Light or medium green. Rnd 10: Beige.

Square B2 (make 6): Follow directions for square B and work colors as follows: Rnds 1 and 2: Light green or medium green. Rnds 3-7: Beige. On rnd 6, work bobbles with apricot. Rnd 8: Cream. Rnd 9: Beige. Rnd 10: Light green or medium green.

Assembly: Referring to diagram for placement, holding 2 squares with wrong sides facing and working through both pieces, join pastel blend with sl st in any corner, * ch 1, sk 1 st, sc in next st, rep from * to next corner. Fasten off. Rep to join squares in vertical rows. Join rows in this same manner.

Border: Rnd 1: Join pastel blend with sl st in any corner, ch 1, * (sc, ch 1, sc) in same st for corner, (sc in next st, ch 1, sk 1 st) to next corner, rep from * around, sl st to first sc.

Rnds 2-4: Ch 1, sc in same st, ch 1, * (sk 1 st, sc in next st, ch 1) to corner, (sc, ch 2, sc) in corner sp, ch 1, rep from * around, sl st to first sc. Fasten off after rnd 4.

Pillow (make 2): Follow directions above to make 5 A2 squares, 1 B1 square, and 2 B2 squares.

Assembly: Each pillow top is 4 blocks square. Arrange 4 squares as desired and join as for afghan above.

Border: Rep rnd 1 as for afghan around each pillow top.

Finishing: *Note:* Use ½″ seam. Cut fabric for front and back of both pillows before cutting bias strips. Cut cording in half.

To make 1 pillow, cut 14″ squares from fabric for front and back. Cut 1¾″-wide bias strips, piecing as needed, to measure 3 yards. Place fabric squares with right sides facing and stitch around 3 sides. Turn and insert pillow form. Turn under seam allowance and slipstitch opening closed. Place crocheted piece right side up on pillow and slipstitch to pillow at seam.

To cover cording, fold bias strip with right sides facing and raw edges aligned. Stitch long edge to form a tube. Turn. Using bodkin or large safety pin, pull cording through tube. Make a knot 6″ from 1 end of piping by first looping piping around 2 fingers 4 times. Bring loose end to back, insert through all loops from left to right, and pull to form a 3-loop knot. Slipstitch knot to corner of pillow, leaving the 6″ tail loose. Slipstitch piping to edge of pillow at seam to the next corner. Tie 2nd knot and continue around in same manner. When you meet 6″ tail, match and slipstitch ends of piping together.

Repeat to make other pillow.

A1	B1	A2	B1	A2	B1	A1
B1	A2	B1	A2	B1	A2	B1
A2	B1	B2	B2	B2	B1	A2
B1	A2	B1	B1	B1	A2	B1
A2	B1	B2	B2	B2	B1	A2
B1	A2	B1	A2	B1	A2	B1
A1	B1	A2	B1	A2	B1	A1

Placement Diagram

Pastel Hearts

Soft pastel hearts framed in dainty white squares make a colorful keepsake throw to shower a new baby with love.

■ ■ ■

FINISHED SIZE
Approximately 46″ x 44″, not including fringe.

MATERIALS
Sportweight cotton: 2 oz. each apricot (A), light yellow (B), light green (C), light blue (D), lavender (E), pink (F).
Sportweight acrylic: 18 oz. white.
Sizes E and F crochet hooks, or sizes to obtain gauge.

GAUGE
Square = 7″.

DIRECTIONS

Heart (make 6 of each color): With size E hook, ch 4, join with a sl st to form a ring.

Row 1: Ch 3 for first dc, work (dc, 3 tr, 7 dc, 3 tr, 2 dc) in ring—17 sts counting beg ch. Ch 1, turn.

Row 2: Sc in same st as ch-1, sc in next st, 2 sc in each of next 2 sts, sc in each of next 3 sts, 3 sc in next st, sc in each of next 3 sts, 2 sc in each of next 2 sts, sc in each of next 2 sts. Ch 3, turn.

Row 3: Dc in each of next 2 sts, 2 dc in each of next 3 sts, dc in each of next 5 sts, 3 dc in next st (point of heart), dc in each of next 5 sts, 2 dc in each of next 3 sts, dc in each of next 2 sts, hdc in next st, (hdc, 2 sc) around post of next dc, (2 sc, hdc) around post of next dc, join with sl st to top of first dc. Fasten off.

Square: Rnd 1: With right side of heart facing and working in bar just below bk lp, use F hook and join white with sl st in 3rd st from center top on left side, (ch 5, sk 1 st, sl st in next bar) 16 times, hdc in first sl st.

Rnd 2: Sc in lp just made, (ch 7, sc in next lp) 15 times, ch 3, tr in first sc.

Rnd 3: Sc in lp just made, * ch 7, sc in next lp, rep from * around, end with ch 7, sl st to first sc.

Rnd 4: Ch 2 for first hdc, 4 hdc in next lp, hdc in next sc, ch 15 for corner, * sk 2 lps, hdc in next sc, 4 hdc in next lp, hdc in next sc, 4 hdc in next lp, hdc in next sc **, ch 15, rep from * around, end last rep at **, sl st to top of beg ch.

Rnd 5: Ch 2 for first hdc, hdc in each of next 3 sts, dc in next st, * dc in each of next 7 ch, 3 dc in next ch for corner, dc in each of next 7 ch, dc in next hdc, hdc in each of next 3 hdc, dc in each of next 2 sts, hdc in each of next 3 sts, dc in next st, rep from * around, sl st to top of beg ch.

Rnd 6: Ch 3 for first dc, * dc evenly to next corner, 3 dc in center st of corner, rep from * around. Fasten off.

Assembly: With wrong sides facing and referring to placement diagram, whipstitch squares tog through bk lps only, leaving corner dc sts unworked for a small opening at intersections of squares (see photograph).

Border: Rnd 1: Join white with sl st in any corner, ch 3 for first dc, 2 dc in same st, * (dc in each st to 3 sts before joining of squares, tr in each of next 3 sts, sk joining seam, tr in each of next 3 sts) to next corner, work 3 dc in corner, rep from * around afghan, sl st to top of beg ch.

Rnd 2: Ch 3 for first dc, * 3 dc in next st for corner, dc evenly to next corner, rep from * around, sl st to top of beg ch. Fasten off.

Edging: With right side facing and afghan turned to work down 1 side edge, join white with sl st in corner, * sc in next st, hdc in each of next 2 sts, (2 dc, ch 3, sl st in 3rd ch from hook to make a picot, dc) in next st, hdc in each of next 2 sts, sc in next st, rep from * to corner. Fasten off.

Rep edging on rem side edge of afghan. Do not work picot edging on ends of afghan.

Fringe: Cut 2 (9″) strands for each tassel. Use 1 strand of each of the 6 pastel colors with 1 strand of white, or 2 strands of white. Alternate color tassels with white tassels, knotting tassels in each st across top and bottom ends of afghan (see photograph).

A	B	C	D	E	F
B	C	D	E	F	A
C	D	E	F	A	B
D	E	F	A	B	C
E	F	A	B	C	D
F	A	B	C	D	E

Placement Diagram

Cozy Colors

Arrange a rainbow of hues for an afghan of many colors.

■ ■ ■

FINISHED SIZE
Approximately 51″ x 66″, not including fringe.

MATERIALS
Worsted-weight acrylic: 3 oz. each light green (A), medium green (B), dark green (C), dark jade (D); 7 oz. each medium jade (E), jade (F), light aqua (G); 10 oz. each medium aqua (H), dark aqua (I), very light blue (J), light blue-gray (K), medium blue-gray (L), light powder blue (M), medium blue (N), dark blue (O); 7 oz. each light purple (P), medium purple (Q), dark purple (R); 3 oz. each dark plum (S), medium plum (T), light plum (U), very light plum (V).
Size G crochet hook, or size to obtain gauge.

GAUGE
Square = 5″.

DIRECTIONS
Square (make 130 referring to placement diagram for color): Ch 4, join with a sl st to form a ring.
Rnd 1: Ch 3 for first dc, 11 dc in ring, sl st to top of beg ch — 12 dc counting beg ch.
Rnd 2: Ch 2 for first hdc, keeping last lp of each st on hook, work 3 hdc in same st, yo and through all lps on hook (beg puff st completed), * ch 5 for corner, [keeping last lp of each st on hook, work 4 hdc in next dc, yo and through all lps on hook (puff st completed), ch 1] twice, puff st in next st, rep from * twice more, ch 5 for corner, (puff st, ch 1) twice, sl st to first puff st — 12 puff sts.
Rnd 3: Sl st in next sp, ch 3 for first dc, 4 dc in same corner, * ch 2, puff st in next sp, ch 1, puff st in next sp, ch 2 **, 5 dc in next corner, rep from * around, end last rep at **, sl st to top of beg ch.
Rnd 4: Ch 4 for first dc and ch 1, dc in next dc, ch 1, * (dc, ch 1) 3 times in next dc for corner, dc in next dc, ch 1, dc in next dc, ch 2, puff st in next sp, ch 2 **, (dc in next dc, ch 1) twice, rep from * around, end last rep at **, sl st to top of beg ch.
Rnd 5: Ch 3 for first dc, * dc in each sp and dc to center st of next corner, 3 dc in corner, rep from * around, sl st to top of beg ch.

Rnd 6: Ch 1, * sc in each st to next corner, 3 sc in next corner, rep from * around, sl st to first sc. Fasten off.

Assembly: With wrong sides facing and referring to diagram for placement, whipstitch squares tog through bk lps only.

Border: Using yarn colors as desired, join yarn with sl st in any corner of afghan, ch 3 for first dc, 2 dc in same corner, * (dc in each st to 1 st before joining of squares, tr in corner of square, tr in joining seam, tr in corner of next square) to next corner of afghan, 3 dc in corner of afghan, rep from * around, sl st to top of beg ch. Fasten off.

Fringe: For each tassel, cut 16 (12″) strands. Make 4 tassels of each color except K and L. Matching tassels to squares, knot tassels across ends of afghan. Make a 2nd row of knots in fringe by knotting tog 8 strands from 1 tassel and 8 from the next tassel about 1″ below the first knot.

J	I	H	G	F	E	D	C	B	A
K	J	I	H	G	F	E	D	C	B
L	K	J	I	H	G	F	E	D	C
M	L	K	J	I	H	G	F	E	D
N	M	L	K	J	I	H	G	F	E
O	N	M	L	K	J	I	H	G	F
P	O	N	M	L	K	J	I	H	G
Q	P	O	N	M	L	K	J	I	H
R	Q	P	O	N	M	L	K	J	I
S	R	Q	P	O	N	M	L	K	J
T	S	R	Q	P	O	N	M	L	K
U	T	S	R	Q	P	O	N	M	L
V	U	T	S	R	Q	P	O	N	M

Placement Diagram

Granny's Favorites

Borrow a quilt pattern to crochet this nine-patch block.

■ ■ ■

FINISHED SIZE
Afghan: Approximately 35″ x 52″.
Pillow: Approximately 18″ square.

MATERIALS
Worsted-weight acrylic: 26 oz. lavender; 9 oz. each pink, blue, orchid; 2 oz. gray.
Size G crochet hook, or size to obtain gauge.
1¾ yards (45″-wide) pink fabric.
Thread to match.
3⅔ yards (1″) cording.
18″-square pillow form.

GAUGE
Afghan square = 2½″.
Pillow square = 9″.

DIRECTIONS
Afghan square (make 72 each of pink, blue, and orchid): *Note:* Rnd 4 border is always worked with lavender.

With first color, ch 6, join with a sl st to form a ring.

Rnd 1: Sc in ring, (ch 2, sc in ring) 7 times, ch 2, sl st to first sc.

Rnd 2: Sl st in next sp, 3 sc in sp for corner, ch 2, * sc in next sp, ch 2, 3 sc in next sp for corner, rep from * around, ch 2, sl st to first sc.

Rnd 3: Sl st to center st of 3-sc group, ch 3 for first dc, 2 dc in same st, * (ch 2, dc in next ch-2 sp) twice, ch 2 **, 3 dc in center st of 3-sc group for corner, rep from * around, end last rep at **, sl st to top of beg ch. Fasten off.

Rnd 4 (border rnd): Join lavender in center st of any corner, ch 3 for first dc, 2 dc in same st, * (ch 2, dc in next ch-2 sp) 3 times, ch 2 **, 3 dc in center st of next corner, rep from * around, end last rep at **, sl st to top of beg ch. Fasten off.

Nine-patch block assembly (make 24): Use 3 squares each of pink, blue, and orchid to make a block. Arrange squares in a block 3 squares wide and 3 squares long (see photograph for color placement). With right sides facing and lavender, sl st squares tog through bk lps only.

Border: Rnd 1: Join lavender in any corner, * 3 sc in corner, sc evenly to next corner, rep from * around, sl st to first sc.

Rnds 2 and 3: Working in bk lps only, rep rnd 1. Fasten off after rnd 3.

Assembly: Afghan is 4 blocks wide and 6 blocks long. With right sides facing and lavender, sl st blocks tog.

Border: Join lavender in any corner, * 3 sc in corner, sc evenly to next corner, rep from * around, sl st to first sc. Fasten off.

Pillow square (make 4): With orchid, ch 6, join with a sl st to form a ring.

Rnd 1: Ch 5 for first dc and ch 2, (dc in ring, ch 2) 15 times, sl st to 3rd ch of beg ch—16 sts counting beg ch.

Rnd 2: Ch 7 for first tr and ch 3, * tr in next sp, ch 3, rep from * around, sl st to 4th ch of beg ch. Fasten off.

Rnd 3: Join gray in any ch-3 sp, ch 3 for first dc, dc in same sp, * ch 2, 2 dc in next sp, rep from * around, sl st to top of beg ch. Fasten off.

Rnd 4: Join lavender in any ch-2 sp, sc in same sp, * ch 6, sc in next sp, rep from * around, ch 6, sl st to first sc.

Rnd 5: Sl st in next ch-6 sp, * (sc, 5 dc, sc) in next ch-6 sp for corner, (sc, 3 dc, sc) in each of next 3 ch-6 sps, rep from * around, sl st to first sc. Fasten off.

Rnd 6: Holding ruffle to front of work, join blue in first sc before corner, sc in same st, * ch 7, sc in next sc, rep from * around, sl st to first sc.

Rnd 7: Sl st in next ch-7 lp, ch 3 for first dc, 6 dc in same lp for corner, * (ch 2, 3 dc in next lp) 3 times, ch 2 **, 7 dc in next lp for corner, rep from * around, end last rep at **, sl st to top of beg ch.

Rnd 8: Ch 1, working in bk lps only, sc in each of next 3 dc, 3 sc in center dc of 7-dc group for corner, sc in each of next 3 dc, * (ch 2, sc in each of next 3 dc) 3 times, ch 2 **, sc in each of next 3 dc, 3 sc in next dc for corner, sc in each of next 3 dc, rep from * around, end last rep at **, sl st to first sc.

Rnd 9: Sl st in next 2 sc, ch 3 for first dc, working in bk lps only, dc in next sc, 3 dc in corner sc, dc in each of next 2 sc, * (ch 3, 2 dc in next sp) 4 times, ch 3, sk next 2 sc, dc in each of next 2 sc, 3 dc in corner, dc in each of next 2 sc, rep from * around, sl st to top of beg ch. Fasten off.

Rnd 10: Join gray in center st of any corner, ch 3 for first dc, 2 dc in same corner, * sk next dc, dc in each dc and sp to 1 st before next corner, sk 1 st, 3 dc in corner, rep from * around, sl st to top of beg ch. Fasten off.

Rnd 11: Join pink in any corner, sc in corner, ch 3, sc in same st, * (ch 3, sk 2 dc, sc in next dc) 9 times, ch 3, sk 2 dc, (sc, ch 3, sc) in next corner, rep from * around, sl st to first sc.

Rnd 12: Sl st in next sp, * (sc, 3 dc, sc) in corner, (sc, 2 dc, sc) in each sp to next corner, rep from * around, sl st to first sc. Fasten off.

Rnd 13: Join lavender in any corner, working in bk lps only, * 3 sc in corner, sc in next st, (ch 1, sk 2 sts, sc in each of next 2 dc) to next corner, sc in first st of 3-sc group, rep from * around, sl st to first sc.

Rnd 14: Working in bk lps only, * 3 sc in corner, sc evenly to next corner, rep from * around, sl st to first sc.

Rnds 15 and 16: Rep rnd 14. Fasten off after rnd 16.

Assembly: Pillow top is 4 blocks square. With wrong sides facing and lavender, whipstitch squares tog through bk lps only.

Finishing: *Note:* Use ½″ seam. From fabric, cut 19″ squares for front and back. Cut 2¾″-wide bias strips, piecing as needed, to measure 3⅔ yards.

To cover cording, fold bias strip with right sides facing and raw edges aligned. Stitch long edge to form a tube. Turn. Using a bodkin or large safety pin, pull cording through tube.

With right sides facing, stitch front and back together around 3 sides, rounding corners slightly. Turn and insert pillow form. Turn under seam allowance and slipstitch opening closed. Place the crocheted piece right side up on pillow and slipstitch to pillow at seam.

To attach piping, first tie a knot 6″ from end. Slipstitch knot to corner of pillow, leaving the 6″ tail loose. Slipstitch piping to edge of pillow at seam to the next corner. Tie 2nd knot and continue around in same manner. When you meet 6″ tail, match and slipstitch ends of piping together.

Blanket of Lavender

This lacy square worked with a thick-and-thin linen yarn in purple and blue creates an afghan of exceptional grace.

■ ■ ■

FINISHED SIZE
Approximately 41″ x 63″.

MATERIALS
Sportweight linen-cotton blend thick-and-thin texture: 13 oz. blue; 24 oz. purple.
Size F crochet hook, or size to obtain gauge.

GAUGE
Square = 5½″.

DIRECTIONS
Square A: With purple, ch 6, join with a sl st to form a ring.

Rnd 1: Ch 1, (sc in ring, ch 6) 8 times, sl st to first sc—8 lps.

Rnd 2: Sl st in next 2 ch, ch 4 for first tr, 5 tr in same lp, * ch 3, sc in next lp, ch 3, 6 tr in next lp, rep from * twice more, ch 3, sc in last lp, ch 3, sl st to top of beg ch.

Rnd 3: Ch 3 for first dc, dc in each of next 5 tr, * ch 6, sc in next sc, ch 8, sc in same sc, ch 6 **, dc in each of next 6 tr, rep from * around, end last rep at **, sl st to top of beg ch. Fasten off.

Rnd 4 (joining rnd): **First square:** Join blue with sl st in any ch-8 lp, * sc in lp, ch 5, sc in next lp, ch 5, sk 3 dc, work (2 dc, 1 tr, ch 3, sl st in 3rd ch from hook to make a picot, 2 dc) bet 3rd and 4th sts of 6-dc group for corner, sk next 3 dc, ch 5, sc in next lp, ch 5, rep from * around, sl st to first sc. Fasten off.

Second square: Join blue in any ch-8 lp, sc in lp, ch 5, sc in next lp, ch 5, sk 3 dc, work (2 dc, tr, ch 1) bet 3rd and 4th sts of 6-dc group on 2nd square, sl st in corresponding picot of first square, ch 1, sl st in top of tr on 2nd square, 2 dc in same corner of 2nd square, (ch 2, sl st in next corresponding lp on first square, ch 2, sc in next lp on

2nd square) 3 times, ch 2, sl st in next lp on first square, ch 2, (2 dc, tr, ch 1) bet 3rd and 4th sts of 6-dc group on 2nd square, sl st in corresponding picot on first square, ch 1, sl st in top of tr on 2nd square, 2 dc in same corner on 2nd square, complete square same as first square. Fasten off.

Cont to make and join squares as established, following placement diagram and working colors as follows: Square A: Rnds 1-3, purple; rnd 4, blue. Square B: Rnds 1 and 2, purple; rnds 3 and 4, blue. Square C: Rnd 1, purple; rnds 2-4, blue. Square D: Rnds 1-4, purple.

Edging: Join purple with sl st in any corner, sc in corner, * (ch 5, sc in next lp) 4 times, ch 5, sc in joining of squares, rep from * to next corner, ch 5, sc in corner picot, rep from first * around, end with ch 5, sl st to first sc. Fasten off.

A	A	B	C	B	A	A
D	D	D	D	D	D	D
D	A	B	C	B	A	D
D	A	D	D	D	A	D
D	B	D	D	D	B	D
D	C	D	D	D	C	D
D	B	D	D	D	B	D
D	A	D	D	D	A	D
D	A	B	C	B	A	D
D	D	D	D	D	D	D
A	A	B	C	B	A	A

Placement Diagram

Mosaic Squares

Work yarn colors in different combinations to obtain the mosaic pattern of these squares. Then join a few of the squares to make a scarf for a cherished teddy bear.

FINISHED SIZE
Afghan: Approximately 41″ x 54″.
Teddy bear scarf: Approximately 3¼″ x 34″, not including fringe.

MATERIALS
Fingering-weight cotton: 4 oz. each dark green (A), beige (B), light green (C), light gray (D), medium gray (E), dark gray (F), lavender (G).
Size E crochet hook, or size to obtain gauge.

GAUGE
Square = 3¼″.

DIRECTIONS
Square: With first color, ch 4, join with a sl st to form a ring.

Rnd 1: Ch 3 for first dc, 2 dc in ring, (ch 2 for corner, 3 dc in ring) 3 times, ch 2, sl st to top of beg ch. Fasten off.

Rnd 2: Join next color in any ch-2 corner, ch 3 for first dc, (ch 2, dc) in same corner, * dc in each of next 3 sts, work (dc, ch 2, dc) in corner, rep from * around, sl st to top of beg ch. Fasten off.

Rnd 3: Join next color in any corner, ch 2 for first hdc, (hdc, ch 2, 2 hdc) in same corner, * hdc in each st to next corner, (2 hdc, ch 2, 2 hdc) in corner, rep from * around, sl st to top of beg ch. Fasten off.

Rnd 4: Join next color in any corner, ch 3 for first dc, (dc, ch 2, 2 dc) in same corner, * dc in each st to next corner, (2 dc, ch 2, 2 dc) in corner, rep from * around, sl st to top of beg ch. Fasten off.

Rnd 5: Join next color in any corner, ch 3 for first dc, (dc, ch 2, 2 dc) in same corner, * dc in each st to next corner, (2 dc, ch 2, 2 dc) in corner, rep from * around, sl st to top of beg ch. Fasten off.

Afghan: Rep rnds 1-5 to make 192 squares (32 each of squares 1-6), working colors as follows:

	Rnd 1	Rnd 2	Rnd 3	Rnd 4	Rnd 5
Square 1	A	B	C	D	E
Square 2	F	D	G	B	E
Square 3	B	E	D	C	A
Square 4	F	D	G	C	A
Square 5	A	C	B	D	F
Square 6	G	B	C	D	F

Assembly: Afghan is 12 squares wide and 16 squares long. With wrong sides facing and A, whipstitch squares tog through bk lps only.

Border: Rnd 1: Join A with sl st in any corner, ch 3 for first dc, (2 dc, ch 2, 3 dc) in same sp, * [dc in each of next 17 sts, (2 dc in next sp) twice] to corner, work (3 dc, ch 2, 3 dc) in corner, rep from * around, sl st to top of beg ch.

Rnd 2: Sl st in next sp, ch 3 for first dc, (2 dc, ch 2, 3 dc) in same sp, * (ch 3, sk 3 sts, dc in each of next 3 sts) to corner, ch 3, work (3 dc, ch 2, 3 dc) in corner, rep from * around, sl st to top of beg ch.

Rnd 3: Sl st in next sp, ch 3 for first dc, (2 dc, ch 2, 3 dc) in same sp, * (3 dc in next sp, ch 3) to corner, omit ch 3 just before corner, work (3 dc, ch 2, 3 dc) in corner, rep from * around, sl st to top of beg ch.

Teddy bear scarf: Make 3 each of squares 1, 3, and 5 as established.

Assembly: Whipstitch squares tog with A to make a row of 9 squares.

Edging: Work edging on long edges of scarf only. With right side facing, join A in corner, ch 1, sc evenly to next corner, fasten off. Rep for other long edge.

Fringe: For each tassel, cut 1 (10″) strand of each color. Knot 7 tassels evenly across each end of scarf.

Country Squares

Work soft cotton yarns into this reversible square. On one side, the post stitches make a raised circle design, while on the other, a swirl pattern appears.

FINISHED SIZE
Approximately 45″ x 63″.

MATERIALS
Worsted-weight cotton: 20 oz. each beige, taupe.
Size J crochet hook, or size to obtain gauge.

GAUGE
Square = 5″.

DIRECTIONS
Square (make 88): With beige, ch 6, join with a sl st to form a ring.

Rnd 1: Ch 3 for first dc, 15 dc in ring, sl st to top of beg ch. Fasten off.

Rnd 2: Make a sl knot with taupe, yo and insert hook from behind and from right to left around post of any dc on rnd 1, complete st as a dc (beg dc/raised back completed), yo and insert hook from behind and from right to left around same dc post, complete st as a dc (1 dc/rb completed), * ch 3, sk 1 dc, 2 dc/rb around post of next dc on rnd 1, rep from * around, end with ch 3, sl st to top of beg ch. Fasten off.

Rnd 3: Join beige with sl st in any ch-3 sp, ch 3 for first dc, work (dc, ch 3, 2 dc) in same sp for corner, * 3 dc in next ch-3 sp, (2 dc, ch 3, 2 dc) in next sp for corner, rep from * twice more, 3 dc in last ch-3 sp, sl st to top of beg ch. Fasten off.

Rnd 4: Join taupe with sl st in any corner, ch 2 for first hdc, work (hdc, ch 2, hdc) in same corner, * hdc in each of next 7 sts, work (2 hdc, ch 2, 2 hdc) in corner, rep from * twice more, hdc in each of last 7 sts, sl st to top of beg ch. Fasten off.

Rnd 5: Join beige in any corner, ch 3 for first dc, work (dc, ch 2, 2 dc) in same corner, * dc in each of next 11 sts, (2 dc, ch 2, 2 dc) in next corner, rep from * around, dc in each of last 11 sts, sl st to top of beg ch. Fasten off.

Assembly: Afghan is 8 squares wide and 11 squares long. With wrong sides facing and beige, whipstitch squares tog through bk lps only.

Border: Rnd 1: Join taupe in any corner, ch 3 for first dc, work (dc, ch 2, 2 dc) in same corner, dc in each of next 2 sts, * (ch 1, sk 1 st, dc in next st) to 2 sts before next corner, dc in each of next 2 sts, work (2 dc, ch 2, 2 dc) in corner, rep from * around, sl st to top of beg ch.

Rnd 2: Ch 3 for first dc, * dc in each dc to corner sp, work (2 dc, ch 2, 2 dc) in corner, dc in each of next 4 dc, (ch 1, dc in next dc) to 4 dc before next corner sp, ch 1, rep from * around, sl st to top of beg ch. Fasten off.

Rnd 3: Join beige in any corner, ch 3 for first dc, work (dc, ch 2, 2 dc) in same corner, dc in each of next 6 dc, (ch 1, dc in next dc) to 6 dc before next corner, ch 1, dc in each of next 6 dc, work (2 dc, ch 2, 2 dc) in corner, rep from * around, sl st to top of beg ch. Fasten off.

Rnd 4: Join taupe in any corner, ch 3 for first dc, work (dc, ch 2, 2 dc) in same corner, * dc in each of next 8 dc, (ch 1, dc in next dc) to 8 dc before next corner, ch 1, dc in each of next 8 dc, work (2 dc, ch 2, 2 dc) in corner, rep from * around, sl st to top of beg ch. Fasten off.

Shades of the Southwest

Bring a touch of the Southwest into your sitting room by stitching these squares in colors reminiscent of the desert.

■ ■ ■

FINISHED SIZE
Approximately 39″ x 50″.

MATERIALS
Sportweight acrylic with colored puffs: 11 oz. multicolor pastel.

Sportweight brushed acrylic: 11 oz. light orange; 6 oz. each medium orange, dark orange.

Size H crochet hook, or size to obtain gauge.

GAUGE
Square = 5½″.

DIRECTIONS
Note: The orange yarns are used alternately to work rectangles of 12 sts and 4 rows randomly placed in each square. Some of the rectangles are centered in the square, some are at the edge of the square, and some are located a few sts in from the edge (see photograph).

To avoid holes when changing colors, bring up new color from under dropped color. Always bring up new color as last yo of old color. Carry multicolor yarn across the row by working over it with the next group of sts. Drop orange yarn to back of work and pick it up as needed on later rows.

Square (make 48): With multicolor pastel, ch 21.

Row 1: Hdc in 2nd ch from hook and in each st across. Turn.

Row 2: Ch 2 for first hdc, hdc in each st across. Turn.

Row 3: Ch 2 for first hdc, hdc in next 5 sts, join light orange and work 12 hdc, change to multicolor pastel and hdc in each of rem sts. Turn.

Rows 4-6: Rep row 3 working colors as established. Fasten off light orange after row 6.

Rows 7-14: Hdc in each st across, ch 2, turn. Fasten off after row 14.

Rep directions above, using orange yarns as follows: 16 light orange rectangles, 17 medium orange rectangles, and 15 dark orange rectangles.

Border: Join light orange in any corner, * work 3 sc in corner, sc evenly to next corner, rep from * around, sl st to first sc. Fasten off.

Assembly: Afghan is 6 squares wide and 8 squares long. Arrange squares as desired (see photograph). With wrong sides facing and light orange, whip-stitch squares tog through bk lps only.

Edging: Rnd 1: Join light orange with sl st in any corner, ch 4 for first dc and ch 1, dc in same st, * (ch 1, sk 1 st, dc in next st) to corner, ch 1, (dc, ch 1, dc, ch 1, dc) in next corner, rep from * around, end with (dc, ch 1) in beg corner, sl st to 3rd ch of beg ch.

Rnd 2: Sl st to center dc of corner, ch 5 for first dc and ch 2, dc in same st, * (ch 1, dc in next sp) to next corner, ch 1, (dc, ch 2, dc) in center dc of next corner, rep from * around, sl st to 3rd ch of beg ch.

Rnd 3: Sl st in corner sp, ch 6 for first dc and ch 3, dc in same sp, * (ch 1, dc in next sp) to next corner, ch 1, (dc, ch 3, dc) in next corner sp, rep from * around, sl st to 3rd ch of beg ch.

Rnd 4: Sl st in corner sp, ch 3 for first dc, keeping last lp of each st on hook, work 2 dc in same sp, yo and through all lps on hook (beg cluster completed), ch 3, keeping last lp of each st on hook, work 3 dc in same corner sp, yo and through all lps on hook (cluster completed), * (ch 1, cluster in next sp, ch 1, dc in next sp) to sp before next corner, ch 1, cluster in sp before corner, (cluster, ch 3, cluster) in corner, rep from * around, sl st to top of beg cluster.

Rnd 5: Sl st in corner sp, ch 3 for first dc, work beg cluster in same corner, ch 3, cluster in same corner, * ch 1, dc in next cluster, (ch 1, cluster in next cluster, ch 1, dc in next dc) to next corner, (cluster, ch 3, cluster) in corner, rep from * around, sl st to top of beg cluster. Fasten off.

Lacy Linens

...

CHAPTER TWO

Mother's Finest

Entertain in grand style by pairing your finest dinnerware and this striking tablecloth.

■ ■ ■

FINISHED SIZE
Approximately 35″ x 35″.

MATERIALS
Size 10 crochet thread: 10 (250-yd.) balls cream.
Size #7 steel crochet hook, or size to obtain gauge.

GAUGE
Large motif = 5″ diameter.
Small motif = 2¾″ diameter.

DIRECTIONS
Large motif (make 49): Ch 8, join with a sl st to form a ring.

Rnd 1: Ch 5 for first dc and ch 2, (dc in ring, ch 2) 11 times, sl st to 3rd ch of beg ch—12 sps around.

Rnd 2: Sl st in next sp, ch 1, 3 sc in each sp around, sl st to first sc—36 sc.

Rnd 3: Ch 1, working in bk lps only, sc in each st around, sl st to first sc.

Rnd 4: Ch 4 for first dc and ch 1, working in bk lps only, * dc in next st, ch 1, rep from * around, sl st to 3rd ch of beg ch.

Rnd 5: Sl st in next sp, ch 1, work 2 sc in each sp around, sl st to first sc.

Rnd 6: Ch 4 for first tr, working in bk lps only, tr in each of next 4 sts, * ch 5, sk next st, tr in each of next 5 sts, rep from * around, sl st to top of beg ch—12 groups of 5 tr each.

Rnd 7: Ch 1, working in bk lps only, * sc in each of next 5 tr, (4 sc, ch 4, 4 sc) in ch-5 sp, rep from * around, sl st to first sc.

Rnd 8 (joining rnd): **First motif:** Sl st in next 2 sts, ch 1, * sc in each of next 2 sts, ch 5, (dc, ch 4, dc) in ch-4 lp, ch 5, sk 5 sc, rep from * around, sl st to first sc. Fasten off.

Second motif: Sl st in next 2 sts, ch 1, * sc in each of next 2 sts, ch 5, dc in next ch-4 lp, ch 2, sl st in corresponding lp of first motif, ch 2, dc in same ch-4 lp on 2nd motif, ch 5, sk 5 sc on first motif, rep from * once more, complete motif same as first motif. Fasten off.

Cont to make and join motifs as established for a tablecloth 7 motifs wide and 7 motifs long.

Small motif (make 36): *Note:* Small motifs are joined in the openings bet rows of large motifs.

Ch 8, join with a sl st to form a ring.

Rnds 1-3: Rep rnds 1-3 of large motif.

Rnd 4 (joining rnd): Ch 1, working in bk lps only, * sc in each of next 4 sc, ch 6, sc in joining of 2 large motifs, ch 6, sk 1 sc on small motif, sc in next sc, 2 sc in next sc, sc in next sc, ch 4, sc in next unattached ch-4 lp on large motif, ch 4, sk 1 sc on small motif, rep from * around, sl st to first sc. Fasten off.

Dresden Kitchen

For your kitchen, stitch a set of linens that coordinate with your china.

■ ■ ■

FINISHED SIZE
Napkin ring: Approximately 4½″ square.
Place mat: Approximately 17½″ x 25½″.

Towel: Approximately 19″ x 28″.
Shelf liner: Approximately 33″ x 18″.

MATERIALS
Worsted-weight cotton: 4 oz. each white, light blue, medium blue.
Size F crochet hook, or size to obtain gauge.
1 yard (45″-wide) white fabric.
Thread to match.
½ yard heavy-weight interfacing.
2⅓ yards (1″) cording.
Size 10 crochet thread: 1 (282-yd.) ball each white, light blue, medium blue.
Size #7 steel crochet hook, or size to obtain gauge.
1¼ yards (45″-wide) white linen.
1⅞ yards (⅛″-wide) medium blue satin ribbon.
2 yards (⅛″-wide) light blue satin ribbon.

GAUGE

Large square = 4½".
Small square = 2¼".

DIRECTIONS

Square: With white, ch 8, join with a sl st to form a ring.

Rnd 1: Ch 3 for first dc, 2 dc in ring, ch 3, (3 dc in ring, ch 3) 3 times, sl st to top of beg ch.

Rnd 2: Sl st in next sp, ch 3 for first dc, (2 dc, ch 3, 3 dc) in same sp, yo and insert hook from in front and from right to left around post of next dc, complete st as dc (1 dc/raised front completed), 1 dc/rf around each of next 2 dc posts, * (3 dc, ch 3, 3 dc) in next sp for corner, 1 dc/rf around each of next 3 dc posts, rep from * around, sl st to top of beg ch. Fasten off.

Rnd 3: Join light blue in any corner sp, ch 3 for first dc, (2 dc, ch 3, 3 dc) in same sp, * yo and insert hook from behind and from right to left around post of next dc, complete st as dc (1 dc/raised back completed), 1 dc/rb around each of next 2 dc posts, 1 dc/rf around each of next 3 dc posts, 1 dc/rb around each of next 3 dc posts, (3 dc, ch 3, 3 dc) in next corner, rep from * around, sl st to top of beg ch. Fasten off.

Rnd 4: Join medium blue in any corner sp, ch 3 for first dc, (2 dc, ch 3, 3 dc) in same corner, * (1 dc/rf around each of next 3 dc posts, 1 dc/rb around each of next 3 dc posts) twice, 1 dc/rf around each of next 3 dc posts, (3 dc, ch 3, 3 dc) in next corner, rep from * around, sl st to top of beg ch. Fasten off.

Trim: With medium blue, ch 4, join with a sl st to form a ring.

Row 1: Ch 3 for first dc, 6 dc in ring, turn.

Row 2: Ch 5 for first dc and ch 2, sk next dc, 1 dc/raised front around each of next 3 dc posts, ch 2, sk next dc, dc in last st, turn.

Row 3: Ch 5 for first dc and ch 2, 1 dc/rf around each of next 3 dc posts, ch 2, dc in 3rd ch of row 2 beg ch, turn.

Rep rows 2 and 3 for desired length.

Last row: Ch 3 for first dc, keeping last lp of each st on hook, dc in each of next 6 sts, yo and through all lps on hook, ch 1 to tighten. Fasten off.

Napkin ring: Make 2 large squares with worsted-weight cotton yarn and size F hook.

Finishing: Place squares with wrong sides facing. Mark square 2" above and 2" below left-hand corner (see photograph). Stitch the squares together between marks. Repeat for opposite corner.

To make a matching napkin, cut a 16" square from white linen. Turn under ¼" twice around all edges of linen and stitch for hem. Slipstitch a 6½" piece of medium blue ribbon and a 7½" piece of light blue ribbon diagonally across 1 corner of napkin (see photograph).

Place mat: Make 3 large squares with worsted-weight cotton yarn and size F hook. Make a 15" length of trim with worsted-weight cotton yarn and size F hook.

Finishing: *Note:* Use ¼" seam. Cut 2 (24½" x 16½") pieces from white fabric and 1 piece from interfacing. Round all corners. From remaining white fabric, cut 2½"-wide bias strips, piecing as needed, to measure 2⅓ yards.

To cover cording, fold bias strip with right sides facing and raw edges aligned. Stitch long edge to form a tube. Turn. Using bodkin or large safety pin, pull cording through tube.

Layer mat front right side up, mat back right side down, and interfacing. Stitch, leaving an 8" opening. Trim seams and clip curves. Turn. Slipstitch opening closed.

Referring to photograph for placement, slipstitch crocheted squares close to right edge of mat. Slipstitch crocheted trim close to left edge of mat. Slipstitch piping along edge of mat at seam.

Towel: Make 9 small squares with size 10 thread and size #7 hook. Make a 20" length of trim with size 10 thread and size #7 hook.

Assembly: With wrong sides facing, whipstitch 2 squares tog through bk lps only. Rep to join a 3rd square to form a V-shaped piece (see photograph).

Rep to make 3 pieces of 3 squares each.

Finishing: Cut a 20½" x 25" rectangle from white linen. Turn under ¼" twice on all edges and stitch for hem. Slipstitch a 20" length of crocheted trim to towel, 3½" from 1 narrow edge. Referring to photograph for placement, slipstitch a 20" piece each of light blue and medium blue ribbons to towel. Tack corners of crocheted squares to same edge of towel (see photograph).

Shelf liner: Make 15 small squares with size 10 thread and size #7 hook.

Assembly: With wrong sides facing, whipstitch 2 squares tog through bk lps only. Rep to join a 3rd

square to form a V-shaped piece (see photograph). Rep to make 5 pieces of 3 squares each.

Finishing: Cut a 15″ x 34″ rectangle from white linen. Turn under ¼″ twice on all edges and stitch for hem. Referring to photograph for placement, slipstitch a 34″ piece each of light blue and medium blue ribbons close to 1 long edge of shelf liner. Tack corners of crocheted squares to same edge of shelf liner (see photograph).

Basket Liner

Three sizes of flowers, stitched with variegated yellow thread, border a piece of linen to make a unique basket liner.

■ ■ ■

FINISHED SIZE
Approximately 15″ x 20½″.

MATERIALS
5″ x 10″ white linen oval.
Size 30 crochet thread: 6 (350-yd.) balls white; 4 (250-yd.) balls variegated yellow; 2 (250-yd.) balls variegated green.
Size #12 steel crochet hook, or size to obtain gauge.

GAUGE
Small flower square = 3″.

DIRECTIONS

Basket liner: Turn edge of linen under ⅛″ and press.

Rnd 1: With white, work 360 sc sts through fabric and over hem, evenly spaced around edge, join with a sl st to first sc.

Rnd 2: Ch 6 for first dc and ch 3, * sk 2 sts, dc in next st, ch 3, rep from * around, sl st to 3rd ch of beg ch — 120 sps around.

Rnd 3: Sl st in next sp, ch 3 for first dc, (2 dc, ch 5, sl st in 5th ch from hook to make a picot, 3 dc) in same sp, * sc in next sp, (3 dc, picot, 3 dc) in next sp, rep from * around, sc in last sp, sl st to top of beg ch. Fasten off. Set aside.

Small flower square (make 6): With variegated yellow, ch 6, join with a sl st to form a ring.

Rnd 1: Ch 5 for first dc and ch 2, (dc in ring, ch 2) 7 times, sl st to 3rd ch of beg ch.

Rnd 2: Ch 1, (sc, 5 dc, sc) in each sp around, sl st to first sc — 8 petals around.

Rnd 3: Holding petals to front of work, * ch 4, sc from back of work in next dc of rnd 1, rep from * around, sl st to base of beg ch.

Rnd 4: Ch 1, (sc, 7 dc, sc) in each lp around, sl st to first sc.

Rnd 5: Holding petals to front of work, * ch 5, sc from back of work bet next 2 petals, rep from * around, sl st to base of beg ch.

Rnd 6: Ch 1, (sc, 9 dc, sc) in each lp around, sl st to first sc.

Rnd 7: Holding petals to front of work, * ch 6, sc from back of work bet next 2 petals, rep from * around, sl st to base of beg ch.

Rnd 8: Ch 1, (sc, 11 dc, sc) in each lp around, sl st to first sc. Fasten off.

Leaves: Join green with sl st in any sc bet petals, ch 1, sc in same st, (ch 9, sc in 3rd ch from hook, hdc in next ch, dc in each of next 5 ch, sc in same st as first sc), ch 12, sc in 3rd ch from hook, hdc in next ch, dc in each of next 8 ch, sc in same st as first sc, rep bet ( ) once more (3 leaves made). Fasten off. * Sk sc bet next 2 petals, make 3 leaves as before in next sc bet 2 petals, rep from * 3 times more for 4 groups of 3 leaves each.

Edging: Rnd 1: Join white in tip of any center leaf, sc in same st, ch 8, sc in tip of next leaf, * ch 17, sc in sc bet next 2 petals of flower, ch 8, sc in 9th ch of ch-17 just made, (ch 8, sc in tip of next leaf) 3 times, rep from * around, sl st to first sc.

Rnd 2: Ch 8 for first dc and ch 5, dc in same st, * (ch 2, sk 2 sts, dc in next st) 12 times, ch 5, dc in same st for corner, rep from * around, sl st to 3rd ch of beg ch.

Rnd 3: Ch 8 for first dc and ch 5, dc in same st, * (ch 2, dc in next dc) to next corner, work (dc, ch 5, dc) in corner, rep from * around, sl st to 3rd ch of beg ch.

Rnd 4: Rep rnd 3. Fasten off.

Medium flower square (make 4): **Rnds 1-8:** Work as for small flower square rnds 1-8.

Rnd 9: Holding petals to front of work, * ch 7, sc from back of work bet next 2 petals, rep from * around, sl st to base of beg ch.

Rnd 10: Ch 1, (sc, 13 dc, sc) in each lp around, sl st to first sc. Fasten off.

Leaves: Join green with sl st in any sc bet petals, ch 1, sc in same st, (ch 12, sc in 3rd ch from hook, hdc in next ch, dc in each of next 8 ch, sc in same st as first sc), ch 15, sc in 3rd ch from hook, hdc in next ch, dc in each of next 11 ch, sc in same st as first sc, rep bet ( ) once more (3 leaves made). Fasten off. * Sk sc bet next 2 petals, make 3 leaves as before in next sc bet 2 petals, rep from * 3 times more for 4 groups of 3 leaves each.

Edging: Rnd 1: Join white in tip of any center leaf, sc in same st, ch 11, sc in tip of next leaf, * ch 24, sc in sc bet next 2 petals of flower, ch 12, sc in 13th ch of ch-24 just made, (ch 11, sc in tip of next leaf) 3 times, rep from * around, sl st to first sc.

Rnd 2: Ch 8 for first dc and ch 5, dc in same st, * (ch 2, sk 2 sts, dc in next st) 16 times, ch 5, dc in same st for corner, rep from * around, sl st to 3rd ch of beg ch.

Rnd 3: Ch 8 for first dc and ch 5, dc in same st, * (ch 2, dc in next dc) to next corner, work (dc, ch 5, dc) in corner, rep from * around, sl st to 3rd ch of beg ch.

Rnd 4: Rep rnd 3. Fasten off.

Basket Liner continued

Large flower square (make 2): **Rnds 1-10:** Work as for medium flower square rnds 1-10.

Rnd 11: Holding petals to front of work, * ch 8, sc bet next 2 petals, rep from * around, sl st to base of beg ch.

Rnd 12: Ch 1, (sc, 15 dc, sc) in each lp around, sl st to first sc. Fasten off.

Leaves: Join green with sl st in any sc bet petals, ch 1, sc in same st, (ch 15, sc in 3rd ch from hook, hdc in next ch, dc in each of next 11 ch, sc in same st as first sc), ch 18, sc in 3rd ch from hook, hdc in next ch, dc in each of next 14 ch, sc in same st as first sc, rep bet ( ) once more (3 leaves made). Fasten off. * Sk sc bet next 2 petals, make 3 leaves as before in next sc bet 2 petals, rep from * 3 times more for 4 groups of 3 leaves each.

Edging: Rnds 1-4: Work as for medium flower square, rnds 1-4.

Assembly: Rnd 1: Join white in any corner of 1 large flower square, ch 3 for first dc, dc in same corner sp, * (2 dc in next sp) to next corner sp, do not fasten off, rep from * across edge of a medium flower square, do not fasten off, rep from * across edge of a small flower square. Cont joining squares as established, in the following order: 2 more small squares, 1 medium square, 1 large square, 1 medium square, 3 small squares, 1 medium square. Join with a sl st to top of beg ch on first large square.

Rnd 2: Ch 4 for first tr, tr in next st, * ch 2, sk 2 dc, tr in each of next 2 dc, rep from * around, sl st to top of beg ch.

Rnd 3: Sl st in next sp, ch 4 for first tr, tr in same sp, * ch 2, sk 2 tr, 2 tr in next sp, rep from * around, sl st to top of beg ch.

Rnd 4: Ch 3 for first dc, * 2 dc in next sp, dc bet next 2 tr, rep from * around, sl st to top of beg ch.

Rnd 5: Ch 6 for first dc and ch 3, sk next 2 dc, dc in next dc, * ch 3, sk next 2 dc, dc in next dc, rep from * around, sl st to 3rd ch of beg ch — 120 sps around. Do not fasten off.

Rnd 6 (joining rnd): Lay assembled squares right side up, insert linen oval in center of squares, with large flower squares at each end of oval. Be sure the center of large squares lines up with center of linen oval. Sl st in next sp, ch 1, sc in same st, * 2 dc in next sp, ch 2, sl st in corresponding picot on linen oval, ch 2, sl st in first ch of ch-2 on square, 2 dc in same sp on square, sc in next sp on square, rep from * around, sl st to first sc. Fasten off.

Flower Coasters

Crochet eight-petal flowers to make a set of decorative coasters. Add a light wash of fabric paint for a touch of color.

■ ■ ■

FINISHED SIZE
Approximately 7″ diameter.

MATERIALS
Size 30 crochet thread: 1 (563-yd.) ball white.
Size #12 steel crochet hook, or size to obtain finished size.
Fabric paints: blue, red.

DIRECTIONS
Coaster: Ch 6, join with a sl st to form a ring.

Rnd 1: Ch 3 for first dc, keeping last lp of each st on hook, work 2 dc in ring, yo and through all lps on hook (beg cluster completed), * ch 3, keeping last lp of each st on hook, work 3 dc in ring, yo and through all lps on hook (cluster completed), rep from * 6 times more, ch 3, sl st to top of first cluster.

Rnd 2: Sl st in next sp, ch 3 for first dc, 7 dc in same sp, * 8 dc in next sp, rep from * around, sl st to top of beg ch — 64 dc counting beg ch.

Rnd 3: Ch 3 for first dc, dc in each dc around, sl st to top of beg ch.

Rnd 4: Ch 3 for first dc, dc in each of next 3 sts, (dc bet next 2 sts, dc in each of next 4 sts, ch 1, dc in each of next 4 sts) 7 times, dc bet next 2 sts, dc in each of next 4 sts, ch 1, sl st to top of beg ch.

Rnd 5: Ch 3 for first dc, dc in each of next 3 sts, * ch 1, dc in next st, ch 1, dc in each of next 4 sts **, ch 1, dc in each of next 4 sts, rep from * around, end last rep at **, sl st to top of beg ch.

Rnd 6: Ch 3 for first dc, dc in each of next 3 sts, * 2 dc in next ch-1 sp, ch 1, dc in next dc, ch 1, 2 dc in next ch-1 sp, dc in each of next 4 sts, ch 1 **, dc in each of next 4 sts, rep from * around, end last rep at **, sl st to top of beg ch.

Rnd 7: Ch 3 for first dc, dc in each of next 5 sts, * 2 dc in next sp, ch 1, sk 1 dc, 2 dc in next sp, dc in

each of next 6 sts, ch 1, sk ch-1 sp, dc in each of next 6 dc, rep from * around, join with sc in top of beg ch.

Rnd 8: Sl st over sc just made, ch 4 for first dc and ch 1, * sk 1 dc, dc in each of next 7 sts, dc in next sp, dc in each of next 8 dc, ch 1, dc in next sp, ch 1, rep from * around, sl st to 3rd ch of beg ch, sl st in next sp.

Note: Now work back and forth in rows to complete each petal, 1 at a time.

Row 1: Ch 3 for first dc, dc in each of next 16 sts, dc in next sp, turn.

Row 2: Ch 3 for first dc, sk 1 st, dc in each of next 14 dc, dc in top of ch-3. Turn.

Row 3: Ch 3 for first dc, sk 1 st, dc in each of next 12 dc, dc in top of ch-3. Turn.

Row 4: Ch 3 for first dc, sk 1 st, dc in each of next 10 dc, dc in top of ch-3. Turn.

Row 5: Ch 3 for first dc, sk 1 st, dc in each of next 8 dc, dc in top of ch-3. Turn.

Row 6: Ch 3 for first dc, sk 1 st, dc in each of next 6 sts, dc in top of ch-3. Turn.

Row 7: Ch 3 for first dc, sk 1 st, keeping last lp of each st on hook, work 1 dc in each of next 4 dc, yo and through all lps on hook, dc in top of ch-3. Turn.

Row 8: Ch 3 for first dc, dc in top of cluster, dc in top of ch-3. Fasten off.

Rep rows 1-8 to complete 7 rem petals. Be sure to beg each petal on right side of work.

Finishing: Use fabric paints to dye coaster. Dilute paint to a watery consistency. Wet coaster with water. Blot excess. With small paintbrush, begin painting in the center of coaster with blue, allowing paint to bleed onto petals. Apply a small amount of red to the tip of each petal and allow to bleed toward center. Stretch coaster on an old towel and pin to shape. Let dry.

Old English Blocks

Inset squares laced with picots combine with ecru linen to drape a favorite table. The picot edging provides a finishing touch.

■ ■ ■

FINISHED SIZE
Approximately 17″ x 43″, not including tassels.

MATERIALS
Size 20 crochet thread: 6 (174-yd.) balls ecru.
Size #10 steel crochet hook, or size to obtain gauge.
17½″ x 43½″ piece of ecru linen.
Thread to match.

GAUGE
Square = 2½″.

DIRECTIONS
Square (make 16): Ch 20.

Row 1: Dc in 8th ch from hook, (ch 2, sk 2 ch, dc in next st) 4 times. Ch 5, turn.

Rows 2-5: * Sk sp, dc in next dc, ch 2, rep from * across. Ch 5, turn. Fasten off after row 5.

Rnd 1: Join thread in any corner, ch 1, (3 sc in next sp) twice, * ch 3, sl st in 3rd ch from hook to make a picot, 3 sc in next sp, picot, 3 sc in next sp, ch 14, turn, sc in 3rd sc before first picot just made, turn, (3 sc, picot) 5 times in lp just made, 3 sc in same lp, 7 sc in corner sp, 3 sc in next sp, rep from * around, end last rep with 4 sc in same corner as beg, sl st to first sc.

Rnd 2: Sc in same st, * (ch 10, sk 1 picot, sc in next picot) twice, ch 10, sc in corner st, rep from * around, sl st to first sc.

Rnd 3: Work * (3 sc, picot) 3 times in next ch-10 lp, 3 sc in same lp, rep from * around, sl st to first sc. Fasten off.

Assembly: Referring to photograph for placement, lay 5 squares in a row with corner picots touching. Tack picots tog. Join a square bet bottom edges of 2nd and 3rd, and 3rd and 4th squares of first row. Join another square bet bottom edges of the 2 squares of prev row.
Rep for 8 rem squares.

Tassels (make 6): For each tassel, cut 48 (6″) strands. Fold strands in half. Tie a piece of thread around strands at fold. Tie another piece of thread tightly around strands about 1″ below fold. Tack a tassel to center picot of bottom corner of first square, center square, and last square on each end of table runner.

Finishing: Place a crocheted piece on 1 end of linen with joined picots ½″ above bottom edge of fabric. Trace around the top of the squares. (This tracing will look like 5 triangles. See photograph.) Remove crocheted piece and cut linen along marked lines for inset. To hem inset, turn under ⅛″ twice, clipping seam allowance as needed. Pin. Repeat for opposite end. Continue folding under seam allowance along long edges of linen. Slip-stitch hem and press. Match crocheted piece to inset. Tack picots to fabric. Repeat for opposite end of table runner.

Edging: With right side of linen facing and piece turned to work down 1 long edge, join thread in corner, ch 1, sc in same place, working sts through fabric and over hem, ch 3, sl st in 3rd ch from hook to make a picot, * 7 sc, picot, rep from * across fabric edge, end with sc in corner. Fasten off.
Rep edging on rem long edge of fabric.

Trousseau Treasure

Star motifs and scallops of triple crochet stitches make a set of mats and napkins to grace the table of a bride.

■ ■ ■

FINISHED SIZE
Place mat: Approximately 12″ x 17″.
Napkin: Approximately 15″ square.

MATERIALS
Size 30 crochet thread: 1 (563-yd.) ball ecru.
Size #12 steel crochet hook, or size to obtain gauge.
16″ square of ecru linen.
Thread to match.

GAUGE
Square = 3½″.

DIRECTIONS
Square (make 7): Ch 6, join with a sl st to form a ring.

Rnd 1: Ch 1, 18 sc in ring, sl st to first sc.

Rnd 2: Ch 5 for first dc and ch 2, dc in same st, ch 1, (sk 2 sts, dc in next st, ch 2, dc in same st, ch 1) 5 times, sl st to 3rd ch of beg ch.

Rnd 3: Ch 3 for first dc, (dc, ch 2, 2 dc) in same sp, sc in next sp, * (2 dc, ch 2, 2 dc) in next sp, sc in next sp, rep from * around, sl st to top of beg ch.

Rnd 4: Sl st in next sp, ch 3 for first dc, (2 dc, ch 1, 3 dc) in same sp, * sc in sp before next sc, sc in sp after sc, (3 dc, ch 1, 3 dc) in next ch-2 sp, rep from * around, sl st to top of beg ch.

Rnd 5: Sl st in next sp, sc in same sp, * ch 11, sk 3 dc and 1 sc, sc in next sc **, ch 11, sk 3 dc, sc in next ch-1 sp, rep from * around, end last rep at **, ch 5, dtr in first sc.

Rnd 6: Ch 4 for first tr, (3 tr, ch 3, 4 tr) in same st, * (4 tr, ch 3, 4 tr) in next ch-11 sp, rep from * around, sl st to top of beg ch.

Rnd 7: Sl st in next sp, sc in same sp, * (ch 10, sc in next sp) twice, ch 13 for corner, sc in next sp, rep from * around, sl st to first sc.

Rnd 8: Ch 3 for first dc, * (6 dc in next ch-10 sp, dc in next sc) twice, 6 dc in next ch-13 sp, (2 dc, ch 2, 2 dc) in center st of same ch-13 sp for corner, 6 dc in same ch-13 sp, rep from * around, sl st to top of beg ch.

Rnd 9: Ch 1, sc in same st, sc in each of next 2 dc, * (ch 5, sl st in 5th ch from hook to make a picot, sc in each of next 3 dc) to next corner, (sc, picot) twice in corner sp, rep from * around, sl st to first sc. Fasten off.

Star motif (make 2): **Rnds 1-4:** Rep directions for square rnds 1-4.

Rnd 5: Sl st in next sp, ch 4 for first tr, (3 tr, ch 3, 4 tr) in same sp, * ch 1, sk 3 dc and 1 sc, sc in next sc, ch 1, sk 3 dc, (4 tr, ch 3, 4 tr) in next sp, rep from * around, sl st to top of beg ch. Fasten off.

Place mat assembly: Row 1: Referring to photograph for placement, arrange 6 squares in 2 rows of 3 each with right sides up and squares turned to form diamonds. Join thread in left-hand corner picot of upper right-hand square, insert hook in corresponding corner picot of next square to the left and join to first square with a sl st. Ch 4 for first tr, (3 tr, ch 3, 4 tr) in same st, sl st in next picot of 2nd square, turn.

Row 2: Ch 4, sl st to next picot of 2nd square, 3 tr in first ch of beg ch-4, (4 tr, ch 3, 4 tr) in next ch-3 sp (shell completed), 4 tr in next picot of first square, sl st in next picot of same square, turn.

Row 3: Ch 3, sl st in next picot of same square, ch 11, sc bet shells, ch 11, sc in ch-3 sp of next shell, ch 11, sc bet next shells, ch 5, dtr in next picot of 2nd square, turn.

Row 4: Ch 5, sk next picot, sl st in next picot of same square, 3 tr in first ch of ch-5, ch 3, 4 tr in same st, * (4 tr, ch 3, 4 tr) in 6th ch of next ch-11 lp, rep from * twice more, ch 1, sk 1 picot, sl st in next picot of first square, ch 3, turn.

Row 5: Sl st in next picot of same square, (ch 11, sc in next ch-3 sp) 4 times, ch 5, dtr in next picot of 2nd square, turn.

Row 6: Ch 5, sk next picot, sl st in next picot of same square, 3 tr in first ch of ch-5, ch 3, 4 tr in same st, * (4 tr, ch 3, 4 tr) in 6th ch of next ch-11 lp, rep from * 3 times more, ch 1, sk 1 picot, sl st in next picot of first square. Fasten off.

Rep rows 1-6 as established 5 times more to join all squares (see photograph). Tack adjacent picots of center squares tog.

To join star motifs in center of place mat: Join thread in center picot on any side of opening, ch 6, sl st in 3rd ch from hook to make a picot, ch 3, sl st in ch-sp of star motif. Fasten off. Rep to join star motif on 4 sides (see photograph). Rep for other star motif.

Edging: Rnd 1: Join thread in ch-3 sp of top right-hand shell, * (ch 13, sc in ch-3 sp of next shell) 4 times, ch 13, sc in 2nd picot on corner of next square **, ch 13, sc in next ch-3 sp, rep from * once more, end last rep at **, ch 13, sc in next picot, (ch 13, sk 1 picot, sc in next picot) to next ch-3 sp of shell, rep from first * around place mat, ch 6, dtr in same ch-3 sp as beg.

Rnd 2: Ch 4 for first tr, (3 tr, ch 3, 4 tr) in same st, * ch 1, (4 tr, ch 3, 4 tr) in 7th ch of next ch-13 lp, rep from * around, sl st to top of beg ch.

Rnd 3: Ch 5 for first dtr, * tr in next st, dc in next st, hdc in next st, 2 sc in next ch-3 sp, hdc in next st, dc in next st, tr in next st, dtr in next st, dtr in next ch-1 sp **, dtr in next st, rep from * around, end last rep at **, sl st to top of beg ch.

Rnd 4: Ch 4 for first tr, (3 tr, ch 3, 4 tr) in same st, * sk next 4 sts, 4 tr in next st, sk next 4 sts, (4 tr, ch 3, 4 tr) in next st, rep from * around, sl st to top of beg ch. Fasten off.

Napkin finishing: Cut a 3″ square from 1 corner of linen for inset. To hem inset, fold raw edges under ¼″ twice, clipping seam allowance at inner corner. Pin. Continue folding under seam allowance around sides of napkin. Slipstitch hem and press. Place crocheted square in cutout on right side of linen and slipstitch to napkin.

Pretty & Pink

Begin with centers of variegated pink and then add rounds of pure white to create this feminine doily to accent a springtime table with old-fashioned charm.

■ ■ ■

FINISHED SIZE
Approximately 9″ x 15″.

MATERIALS
Size 30 crochet thread: 1 (250-yd.) ball variegated pink; 2 (350-yd.) balls white.
Size #12 steel crochet hook, or size to obtain gauge.

GAUGE
Large motif = 3″ diameter.

DIRECTIONS
Large motif (make 15): With variegated pink, ch 8, join with a sl st to form a ring.

Rnd 1: Ch 1, 24 sc in ring, sl st to first sc.

Rnd 2: Ch 1, * 3 sc in same st, sc in each of next 5 sts, rep from * around, sl st to first sc—32 sts.

Rnd 3: Ch 1, * 2 sc in same st, sc in each of next 7 sts, rep from * around, sl st to first sc—36 sts.

Rnd 4: Ch 1, * 3 sc in same st, sc in each of next 8 sts, rep from * around, sl st to first sc—44 sts.

Rnd 5: Ch 1, * 2 sc in same st, sc in each of next 10 sts, rep from * around, sl st to first sc—48 sts.

Rnd 6: Ch 1, sc in same st, * ch 4 for corner, sk 2 sts, sc in each of next 10 sts, rep from * around, sl st to first sc.

Rnd 7: Sl st in next sp, ch 3 for first dc, 10 dc in same sp, * sk 1 st, sc in each of next 9 sts, 11 dc in next sp, rep from * around, sl st to top of beg ch. Fasten off.

Rnd 8: Join white in first dc of any corner, ch 5 for first tr and ch 1, (tr in next dc, ch 1) 10 times, * ch 8, sk 9 sts, (tr in next dc, ch 1) 11 times, rep from * around, sl st to 4th ch of beg ch.

Rnd 9: Ch 6 for first tr and ch 2, work (tr in next tr, ch 2) 10 times, * ch 5, sk ch-8 lp, work (tr in next tr, ch 2) 11 times, rep from * around, sl st to 4th ch of beg ch.

Rnd 10 (joining rnd): **First motif:** Ch 7, sl st in 3rd ch from hook to make a picot, (ch 2, tr in next tr, ch 3, sl st in 3rd ch from hook to make a picot) 10 times, * ch 5, sk ch-5 sp, (tr in next tr, picot, ch 2) 11 times, rep from * around, sl st to 4th ch of beg ch. Fasten off.

Second motif: Ch 7, sl st in 3rd ch from hook to make a picot, (ch 2, tr in next tr, ch 3, sl st in 3rd ch from hook to make a picot) 7 times, hold motifs with wrong sides facing, * (ch 2, tr in next tr of 2nd motif, ch 1, sl st in corresponding picot of first motif, ch 1, sl st in top of tr just made on 2nd motif) 3 times, ch 3, rep from * once more, omitting last ch-3, complete motif same as first motif.

Cont to make and join motifs as established for a table runner 3 motifs wide and 5 motifs long.

Tiny motif (make 8): *Note:* Tiny motifs are joined bet rows of large motifs.

With variegated pink, ch 6, join with a sl st to form a ring.

Rnd 1: Ch 1, 16 sc in ring, join with a sl st to first sc. Fasten off.

Rnd 2 (joining rnd): Join white in any st, ch 7, sc in 3rd ch from hook to make a picot, ch 1, tr in next st, ch 1, * sk first unattached picot of group on large motif, sc in next picot, ch 1, sl st in top of tr just made on tiny motif, (ch 1, tr in next st of tiny motif, ch 1, sc in next picot of large motif, ch 1, sl st in top of tr just made) twice, ch 1, tr in next st of tiny motif, ch 3, sc in top of tr just made, ch 1, tr in next st of tiny motif, ch 1, rep from * around, sl st to 4th ch of beg ch. Fasten off.

Blossoms

Join delicate "nanny" squares to make a tea-time table cover.

■ ■ ■

FINISHED SIZE
Approximately 64" x 81".

MATERIALS
Sportweight brushed acrylic: 18 oz. peach (A); 16 oz. pastel ombre (B); 7 oz. aqua (C).

Sizes E and F crochet hooks, or size to obtain gauge.

GAUGE
Square = 12".

DIRECTIONS
Square (make 20): With size F hook and B, ch 8, join with a sl st to form a ring.

Rnd 1: Ch 4 for first tr, tr in ring, ch 3, keeping last lp of each st on hook, work 2 tr in ring, yo and through all lps on hook (cluster completed), (ch 15, cluster, ch 3, cluster) 3 times, ch 15, sl st to top of beg ch. Fasten off.

Rnd 2 (leaves): Sk first 5 ch of any ch-15 lp and join C in 6th ch, * sc in 6th ch and in each of next 3 ch, ch 9, work a 3-dtr cluster in 8th ch from hook, ch 4, sl st in top of cluster to make a picot, ch 8, sl st in base of cluster (leaf made), (ch 8, 3-dtr cluster in 8th ch from hook, picot, ch 8, sl st in base of cluster) twice, sc in same st as first leaf, sc in each of next 4 ch of ch-15 lp, sk 2 sts, ch 2, 7 dtr in next ch-3 sp (scallop completed), ch 2 **, sk 5 ch of next ch-15 lp, rep from * around, end last rep at **, sl st to first sc. Fasten off.

Rnd 3: Join A in picot of any center leaf, sc in same st, ch 12 for first dc and ch 9, sc in picot of next leaf, * ch 9, dc in center dtr of next scallop, ch 9, sc in picot of next leaf, ch 9 **, (dc, ch 11, dc) in picot of next leaf for corner, ch 9, sc in picot of next leaf, rep from * around, end last rep at **, dc in picot of first leaf, ch 6, dtr in 3rd st of beg ch.

Rnd 4: Ch 12 for first dc and ch 9, turn, dc in ch-9 lp, * (ch 9, dc in next lp) to next corner **, ch 11, dc in same corner lp, rep from * around, end last rep at **, ch 9, dc in corner lp, ch 6, dtr in 3rd st of beg ch.

Rnd 5: Ch 4 for first tr, turn, 4 tr in ch-5 sp, * (ch 9, dc in next lp) to next corner **, work (5 tr, ch 11, 5 tr) in corner lp, rep from * around, end last rep at **, ch 9, 5 tr in beg corner, ch 6, dtr in top of beg ch.

Rnd 6: Rep rnd 5. Fasten off.

Rnd 7 (joining rnd): **First square:** Join A in center st of any corner lp, sc in same st, ch 12 for first dc and ch 9, * (dc in next lp, ch 9) to next corner **, (dc, ch 5, dc) in center st of next corner lp, ch 9, rep from * around, end last rep at **, dc, ch 5, sl st to 3rd ch of beg ch. Fasten off.

Second square: Join A in center st of any corner lp, sc in same st, ch 12 for first dc and ch 9, * (dc in next lp, ch 9) to next corner, (dc, ch 5, dc) in corner lp, rep from * to 3rd corner of square, dc in corner lp of 2nd square, ch 2, sl st in center st of corner of first square, ch 2, (dc in same corner of 2nd square, ch 4, dc in next lp of first square, ch 4, dc in next lp of 2nd square) to last corner, ch 2, sl st in center st of corner of first square, dc in 3rd ch of beg ch of 2nd square. Fasten off.

Cont to make and join squares as established for a table cover 4 squares wide and 5 squares long.

Edging: Rnd 1: With size F hook, join B with sl st in any corner, ch 12 for first dc and ch 9, * (dc in next lp, ch 9) to next corner, (dc, ch 9, dc) in corner lp, ch 9, rep from * around, sl st to 3rd ch of beg ch.

Rnd 2 (leaves): Ch 9, 3-dtr cluster in 8th ch from hook, * ch 7, sl st in base of cluster (leaf made), ch 8, 3-dtr cluster in 8th ch from hook, ch 4, sl st in top of cluster to make a picot, ch 7, sl st in base of cluster, ch 8, 3-dtr cluster in 8th ch from hook, ch 7, sl st in base of cluster, sc in first ch of beg ch-9, sc in each of next 5 sts, drop lp from hook **, insert hook in ch at top of 3rd leaf, pick up dropped lp, yo and through all lps on hook, sc in each of next 5 sts, ch 9, 3-dtr cluster in 8th ch from hook, sl st in same place as sc anchoring prev leaf, rep from * around, end last rep at **, insert hook in ch at top of first leaf and in ch at top of last leaf, pick up dropped lp, yo and through all lps on hook, sc in each of last 4 sts, sl st to base of first leaf.

Flower (make 92): With size F hook and B, ch 8, join with a sl st to form a ring.

Rnd 1: Ch 1, 12 sc in ring, sl st to first sc.

Rnd 2: Change to size E hook, working in bk lps only, (ch 2, 2 dc in same st, 2 dc in next st, ch 2, sl st in same st, sl st in next st) 6 times. Cut yarn, leaving a tail to attach flower to block.

Attach a flower to each dtr scallop bet leaves on each square. Attach a flower at each intersection of 4 squares.

Homespun Web

The stitches used in this ornament resemble the delicate tracery of a spider's web.

■ ■ ■

FINISHED SIZE
Approximately 7½″ diameter.

MATERIALS
Size 30 crochet thread: 1 (563-yd.) ball ecru.
Size #12 steel crochet hook, or size to obtain finished size.
Boilable starch.
Clear filament.

DIRECTIONS
Motif: Ch 6, join with a sl st to form a ring.

Rnd 1: Ch 1, 12 sc in ring, sl st to first sc.

Rnd 2: Ch 1, sc in same sc, * ch 3, sc in next sc, rep from * around, ch 3, sl st to first sc.

Rnd 3: Sl st in next ch-3 sp, ch 1, sc in same sp, * ch 5, sc in next sp, rep from * around, ch 3, dc in first sc — 12 lps around.

Rnd 4: * Pull up a ¾″ lp, yo and through lp on hook, insert hook under single back thread, yo and draw through, yo and through both lps on hook (knot st completed), (knot st pulling first lp up ⅜″) twice, make another knot st pulling first lp up ¾″ (4-knot st group completed), sc in same ch-5 sp, 4-knot st group, sc in next ch-5 sp, rep from * around, sl st to first sc — 24 lps around. Fasten off.

Rnd 5: Join thread in center knot of any lp, sc in same st, * ch 5, sc in center knot of next lp, rep from * around, ch 3, dc in first sc.

Rnd 6: Sc in ch-5 lp just made, * ch 5, sc in next lp, rep from * around, ch 3, dc in first sc.

Rnd 7: Sc in lp just made, * work 4-knot st group, sc in same lp, work 4-knot st group, sk next ch-5 lp, sc in next lp, rep from * around, sl st to first sc. Fasten off.

Rnd 8: Join thread in center knot of any lp directly over sk ch-5, sc in same st, * ch 7, sc in center knot of next lp, rep from * around, ch 4, tr in first sc.

Rnd 9: Sc in lp just made, * ch 9, sc in next ch-7 lp, (work knot st pulling first lp up 1″) twice (2-knot st group completed), sc in next ch-7 lp, rep from * around, ch 5, dtr in first sc.

Rnd 10: Sc in lp just made, * ch 9, sc in center knot of next lp, ch 5, sc in same knot, ch 9, sc in next ch-9 lp, rep from * around, sl st to first sc. Fasten off.

Finishing: Prepare starch according to package directions. Soak crocheted piece in starch solution for several minutes. Remove and gently squeeze out excess. Lay piece right side up on an old towel covered with plastic wrap. Beginning at center, stretch piece out to shape and pin, making sure loops are open and points are straight. Let dry completely. Add a piece of clear filament for a hanger.

Loop d'Linen

Frame a circle of linen with lacy loops for a classic doily.

■ ■ ■

FINISHED SIZE
Approximately 8″ diameter.

MATERIALS
3¼″-diameter circle of white linen.
Size 50 crochet thread: 1 (400-yd.) ball white.
Size 30 crochet thread: 10 yards white.
Size #12 steel crochet hook, or size to obtain finished size.

DIRECTIONS
Doily: Turn edge of linen under ⅛″ twice for narrow hem. Press. With size 50 thread and working over hem, (sc, ch 2) around, join with sl st to first sc—approximately 80 sts around.

Edging: Rnd 1: With size 50 thread, join in any lp bet sts, * ch 2, sc in next lp, rep from * around. Do not join but cont to work around in a spiral. *Note:* Place a marker at the end of rnd and move it up as you complete each rnd.

Rnd 2: * Ch 2, sc in next lp, rep from * around.

Rnds 3-6: * Ch 3, hdc in next lp, rep from * around.

Rnd 7: * Ch 4, hdc in next lp, rep from * around.

Rnds 8 and 9: * Ch 5, sc in next lp, rep from * around.

Rnds 10 and 11: * Ch 6, sc in next lp, rep from * around.

Rnd 12: * Ch 7, sc in next lp, rep from * around.

Rnd 13: * Ch 8, sc in next lp, rep from * around.

Rnd 14: * Ch 9, sc in next lp, rep from * around.

Rnd 15: * Ch 10, sc in next lp, rep from * around. Fasten off.

Finishing: With size 30 thread, embroider feather stitches around fabric circle just inside hem.

Victorian Towel Edging

Knot stitches and a picot edging make a square that recalls all the refinement of the Victorian era. Tack the squares to white linen for a special guest towel.

■ ■ ■

FINISHED SIZE
Approximately 19″ x 37″, not including tassels.

MATERIALS
Size 5 pearl cotton thread: 3 (53-yd.) balls white.
Size #5 steel crochet hook, or size to obtain gauge.
1 yard (45″-wide) white linen.
Thread to match.

GAUGE
Square = 5″.

DIRECTIONS
Square (make 3): Ch 6, join with a sl st to form a ring.

Rnd 1: Ch 4 for first tr, tr in ring, ch 8, (2 tr in ring, ch 8) 3 times, sl st to top of beg ch.

Rnd 2: Ch 1, sc in same st, * pull up a ¾″ lp, yo and through lp on hook, insert hook under single back thread, yo and draw through, yo and through both lps on hook (1 knot st completed), make another knot st, sc in next ch-8 lp, make 2 knot sts, sc bet next 2 tr, rep from * around, sl st to first sc.

Rnd 3: Ch 4 for first tr, tr in same st, * ch 3, sc in center knot of next lp, make 2 knot sts, sk next sc, sc in center knot of next lp, ch 3, 2 tr in next sc, rep from * around, sl st to top of beg ch.

Rnd 4: Ch 6 for first dc and ch 3, * dc in next sc, ch 3, (dc, ch 5, dc) in center knot of next lp for corner, ch 3, dc in next sc, ch 3, dc bet 2 tr, ch 3, rep from * around, sl st to 3rd ch of beg ch.

Rnd 5: Sl st in next sp, ch 1, (4 sc in next sp) twice, * 7 sc in next sp for corner, 4 sc in each sp to next corner, rep from * around, sl st to first sc.

Rnd 6: Ch 10 for first tr and ch 6, * sk 8 sc, sc in each of next 3 sc, ch 10; sk 1 sc, sc in each of next 3 sc, ch 6, sk 8 sc **, (tr, ch 5, tr) in top of next dc on rnd 4, ch 6, rep from * around, end last rep at **, tr in same st as beg, ch 5, sl st to 4th ch of beg ch.

Rnd 7: Sl st in next lp, ch 1, sc in same lp, ch 3, sl st in 3rd ch from hook to make a picot, * (sc, picot) twice more in same lp, (4 sc, picot, 4 sc) in next lp, sc in each of next 3 sc, (2 sc, picot) 5 times in corner lp, 2 sc in same lp, sc in each of next 3 sc, (4 sc, picot, 4 sc) in next lp **, sc in next lp, picot, rep from * around, end last rep at **, sl st to first sc. Fasten off.

Assembly: Lay squares on point in a row with right sides up and with corner picots touching. Tack picots tog (see photograph).

Tassels (make 3): For each tassel, cut 20 (11″) strands. Fold strands in half. Tie a piece of thread around strands at fold. Knot another piece of thread tightly around strands about 1″ below fold. Tack a tassel to center picot at bottom corner of each square.

Finishing: *Note:* Use ¼″ seam. Lay crocheted piece flat with tassels at bottom. Measure across the 3 squares; set aside.

From linen, cut 2 pieces 34½″ long and as wide as crocheted piece, plus ½″ for seam allowance. With right sides facing, stitch sides and 1 end, leaving a small opening for turning. Leave the other end open. Do not turn. Center the crocheted piece on the open end of towel with joined picots ½″ above the bottom edge of fabric. Trace around the top of the squares. (This tracing will look like three triangles. See photograph.) Remove crocheted piece and stitch along marked lines. Trim seam to ¼″; discard fabric triangles. Turn towel right side out and slipstitch opening closed. Press. Match crocheted piece to inset. Tack picots to fabric.

Frosted Dresser Scarf

Stitch rounds of shiny multicolor yarn to make this dresser scarf worthy of Grandma's antique furniture.

■ ■ ■

FINISHED SIZE
Approximately 18″ x 50″.

MATERIALS
Sportweight rayon-linen blend: 2 oz. multicolor beige, avocado, and blue (A).
Worsted-weight nylon-cotton blend thick-and-thin texture: 5 oz. multicolor green, gray, and beige (B).
Size E crochet hook, or size to obtain gauge.
1⅝ yards (45″-wide) gray linen.
Thread to match.

GAUGE
Motif = 6″ diameter.

DIRECTIONS
Motif (make 6): With A, ch 9, join with a sl st to form a ring.
Rnd 1: Ch 3 for first dc, 23 dc in ring, sl st to top of beg ch.
Rnd 2: Ch 5 for first dc and ch 2, (sk 1 dc, dc in next dc, ch 2) 11 times, sl st to 3rd st of beg ch.
Rnd 3: Ch 1, sc in same st, * (hdc, 3 dc, hdc) in next ch-2 sp, sc in next dc, rep from * around, sl st to first sc. Fasten off.
Rnd 4 (joining rnd): **First motif:** Join B in center dc of any scallop, sc in same st, ch 5, sl st in 5th ch from hook to make a picot, * ch 1, (dtr, picot) 6 times in center st of next scallop, ch 1, sc in center st of next scallop, ch 3, work (picot, ch 4) twice **, sc in center st of next scallop, picot, rep from * around, end last rep at **, sl st to first sc. Fasten off.

Second motif: Join B with sl st in center dc of any scallop, sc in same st, ch 5, sl st in 5th ch from hook to make a picot, ch 1, (dtr, picot) 5 times in center st of next scallop, * ch 3, sl st in corresponding picot on first motif, ch 2, sc in first st of ch-3 just made, ch 1 **, work last dtr of group on 2nd motif, picot, ch 1, sc in center st of next scallop on 2nd motif, ch 3, picot, ch 2, sl st in corresponding picot on first motif, ch 2, picot, ch 4, sc in center st of next scallop on 2nd motif, picot, ch 1, dtr in center st of next scallop, picot, dtr in same st, rep from * to ** once, complete motif same as first motif. Fasten off.

Cont to make and join motifs as established for 2 rows of 3 motifs each.

Finishing: Cut linen 19″ x 51″. Turn under ¼″ twice on all edges and slipstitch for hem. Press. Place 1 row of crocheted motifs on right side of end of linen scarf, with motif extending 1½″ below bottom hem. Tack crochet to scarf. Repeat for opposite end.

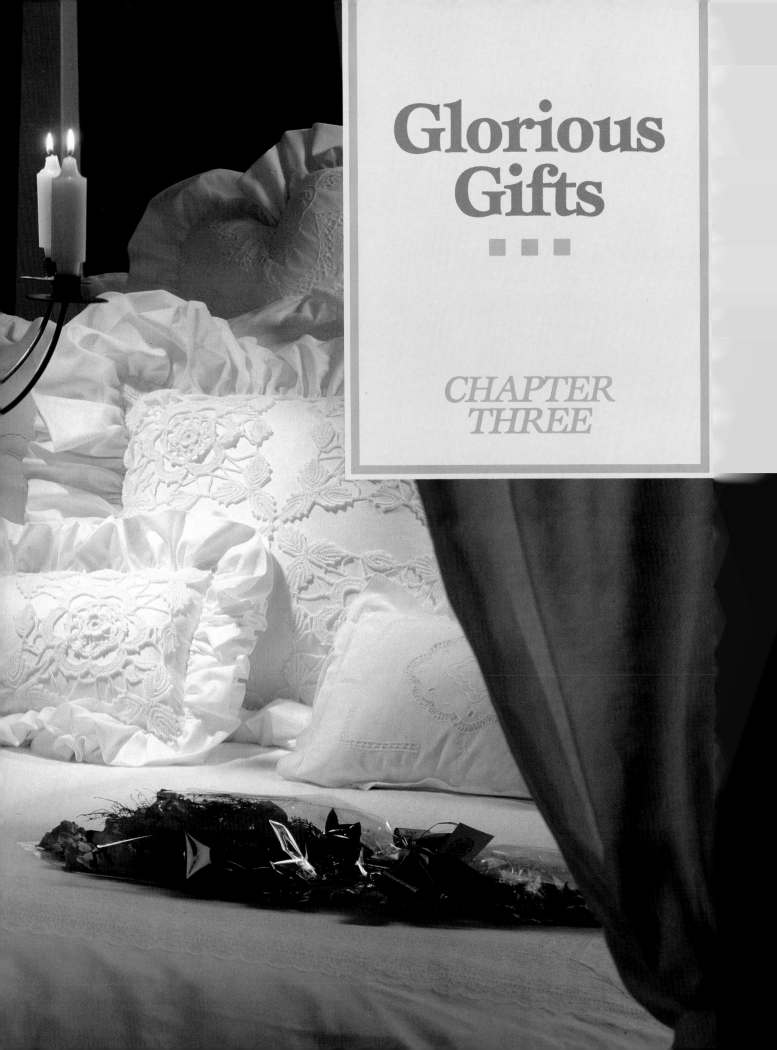

Glorious Gifts

. . .

CHAPTER THREE

The Bridal Suite

Link trefoils of leaves and large roses with chain stitches for a beautiful set of pillows to give a bride-to-be.

■ ■ ■

FINISHED SIZE
Large pillow: Approximately 20″ square, not including ruffle.
Small pillow: Approximately 20″ x 10″, not including ruffle.

MATERIALS
Size 10 crochet thread: 3 (250-yd.) balls white.
Size #10 steel crochet hook, or size to obtain gauge.
9 yards (45″-wide) white fabric.
Thread to match.
Stuffing.

GAUGE
Square = 9″.

DIRECTIONS
Rose motif (make 6): Ch 8, join with a sl st to form a ring.

Rnd 1: Ch 1, 24 sc in ring, sl st to first sc.

Rnd 2: (Ch 4, sk 3 sc, sc in next sc) 6 times, sl st to base of beg ch.

Rnd 3: Work (sc, dc, 3 tr, dc, sc) in each ch-4 lp around, sl st to first sc—6 petals.

Rnd 4: Holding petals to front of work, * ch 5, sc from back of work in next sc bet petals, rep from * around, sl st to first sc.

Rnd 5: Work (sc, dc, 3 tr, dc, sc) in each ch-5 lp around, sl st to first sc.

Rnd 6: * Ch 7, sl st in center st of next petal, ch 7, sl st in st bet next 2 petals, rep from * around, sl st to base of beg ch.

Rnd 7: Sl st to center st of next ch-7 lp, * ch 7, sl st in center st of next ch-7 lp, rep from * around, sl st to base of beg ch.

Rnd 8: Work 7 sc in each ch-7 lp around, sl st to first sc.

Rnd 9: Ch 1, sc in each of 7 sc, * (ch 3, sl st in 3rd ch from hook to make a picot) twice, sc in each of next 14 sc, rep from * around, sl st to first sc.

Rnd 10: (Ch 20, sk 7 sc, 2 picots, and 6 sc, sl st in next sc) 6 times, sl st to base of beg ch.

Rnd 11: Work (sc, 24 tr, sc) in each ch-20 sp around, sl st to first sc.

Rnd 12: * (Sc in each of next 5 sts, picot) 4 times, sc in each of next 5 sts, rep from * around, sl st to first sc. Fasten off.

Large leaf (make 72): Ch 12, sc in 3rd ch from hook, sc in each ch to last ch, 3 sc in last ch, working back along opposite side of ch, sc in each ch to end, turn. * Ch 2, working in bk lps only, sc in each st to center sc at base of leaf, 3 sc in next st, sc in each st to last st, sk last st, rep from * 5 times more for 7 points on leaf. Fasten off.

Small leaf (make 24): Ch 14, sc in 3rd ch from hook, sc in each ch to last ch, 3 sc in last ch, working back along opposite side of ch, sc in each ch to end, turn. * Ch 2, working in bk lps only, sc in each st to center sc at base of leaf, 3 sc in next st, sc in each st to last st, sk last st, rep from * 3 times more for 5 points on leaf.

Joining: Whipstitch 3 large leaves tog at base to make a trefoil for corner of square (see photograph). Make 4 trefoils for each square.

Position rose motif in center, a trefoil in each corner with center leaf pointing away from rose motif, and 4 small leaves bet trefoils with tips pointing clockwise around square (see photograph). *Note:* Be sure to keep ch from twisting while joining pieces.

Join thread with sl st in tip of a small leaf, * ch 4, sl st in tip of next large leaf, ch 13, sl st in 2nd picot of adjacent scallop on rose motif, ch 10, sl st in shortest point on side of same large leaf, ch 10, sl st in 3rd picot on same scallop on rose motif, ch 10, sl st in shortest point on side of next large leaf, ch 10, sl st in last picot on same scallop of rose motif, ch 15, sl st in tip of same large leaf, ch 4, sl st in base of next small leaf, ch 10, sl st in 2nd picot on adjacent rose motif, ch 10, sl st in next picot on same scallop of rose motif, ch 10, sl st in tip of same small leaf, rep from * around as established, end with sl st to base of beg ch.

Rep for rem 5 squares.

Assembly: Large pillow is 4 blocks square. Small pillow is 2 blocks long. Tack tips of center leaves of trefoils tog to join blocks (see photograph).

Finishing: *Note:* Use ½″ seam. Cut fabric for front and back of both pillows before cutting bias strips.

For large pillow, cut 2 (21″) squares from fabric for front and back. For ruffle, cut 11″-wide bias strips, piecing as needed, to measure 12 yards. Cut strip in half widthwise. Fold 1 strip in half lengthwise with right sides facing. Stitch both narrow ends. Turn and press. Stitch gathering threads along raw edges through both layers. Divide strip into fourths and mark. Pin strip to right side of pillow front, aligning raw edges and placing marks at corners. Gather to fit. Stitch. Repeat for remaining strip. Place pillow back over front, with right sides facing and ruffles toward center. Stitch around 3 sides, making sure not to catch ruffles in seam. Turn. Stuff firmly. Turn under seam allowance and slipstitch opening closed. Tack crocheted piece right side up on pillow front.

For small pillow, cut 2 (21″ x 11″) pieces from fabric for front and back. For ruffle, cut 7″-wide bias strips, piecing as needed, to measure 8 yards. Cut in half widthwise and finish strips as above. Mark center of each edge of pillow front. Pin strip to right side of pillow front, aligning raw edges and marks. Finish pillow as above.

Sweet Scents

For thoughtful but easy hostess gifts, fashion sachets in an array of colors and fill them with aromatic potpourri.

■ ■ ■

BLUE SACHET

FINISHED SIZE
Approximately 5″ diameter.

MATERIALS
Size 10 crochet thread: 1 (400-yd.) ball blue.
Size #2 steel crochet hook, or size to obtain gauge.
Scrap of white cotton fabric.
Thread to match.
Small amount of potpourri.
1¼ yards (⅛″-wide) purple satin ribbon.

GAUGE
Motif = 5″ diameter.

DIRECTIONS
Motif (make 2): Ch 6, join with sl st to form a ring.
Rnd 1: Ch 3 for first dc, 11 dc in ring, sl st to top of beg ch.
Rnd 2: Ch 9 for first dc and ch 6, * sk 2 dc, dc in next dc, ch 6, rep from * 4 times more, sl st to 3rd ch of beg ch.
Rnd 3: Ch 3 for first dc, * 7 dc in next sp, dc in next dc, rep from * around, sl st to top of beg ch.
Rnd 4: Sl st in next st, sc in same st, ch 6, * sk 4 dc, sc in next dc, ch 6, rep from * around, sl st to first sc.
Rnd 5: Ch 2 for first hdc, * 7 dc in next sp, hdc in next dc, rep from * around, sl st to top of beg ch.
Rnd 6: Ch 3 for first dc, 2 dc in same st, * ch 3, sk 3 dc, sc in next dc, ch 3, sk 3 dc, 3 dc in next hdc, rep from * around, sl st to top of beg ch.
Rnd 7: Ch 3 for first dc, dc in same st, * ch 3, sk next dc, 2 dc in next dc, ch 3, sk ch-3 sp, dc in next sc, ch 3, sk ch-3 sp, 2 dc in next dc, rep from * around, sl st to top of beg ch.
Rnd 8: Ch 3 for first dc, dc in same st, * sk next dc, ch 3, sc in next ch-3 sp, ch 3, sk next dc, 2 dc in next dc, ch 3, sk ch-3 sp, dc in next dc, ch 3, sk ch-3 sp, 2 dc in next dc, rep from * around, sl st to top of beg ch.
Rnd 9: Sl st in next sp, sc in same sp, * ch 5, sc in next ch-3 sp, rep from * around, sl st to first sc.

Finishing: Cut 2 (3½″) circles from fabric. With right sides facing and using ¼″ seam, stitch together, leaving small opening. Turn and fill with potpourri. Slipstitch opening closed. Place crocheted pieces together with wrong sides facing and stitches aligned. Cut purple ribbon in half. Weave 1 piece of ribbon through rnd-6 beading sps of both pieces to join. Insert sachet before closing completely. Tie ribbon in a bow. Insert remaining ribbon through loop near top and tie in a bow for hanger, if desired. Trim and knot ribbon ends.

GRAY SACHET

FINISHED SIZE
Approximately 5″ diameter.

MATERIALS
Size 5 pearl cotton thread: 1 (53-yd.) ball gray.
Size #7 steel crochet hook, or size to obtain gauge.
Scrap of white cotton fabric.
Thread to match.
Small amount of potpourri.
⅔ yard (¼″-wide) dark blue satin ribbon.

GAUGE
Motif = 5″ diameter.

DIRECTIONS
Motif (make 2): Ch 6, join with a sl st to form a ring.
Rnd 1: Ch 3 for first dc, dc in ring, ch 2, * 2 dc in ring, ch 2, rep from * 4 times more, sl st to top of beg ch.
Rnd 2: Ch 3 for first dc, dc in next dc, * ch 6, dc around post of dc just made, ch 3, dc in each of next 2 dc, rep from * 4 times more, ch 6, dc around post of dc just made, ch 3, sl st to top of beg ch.

Rnd 3: Ch 1, sc in same st, * 7 hdc in next ch-6 sp, 4 sc in next ch-3 sp, rep from * around, sl st to first sc.

Rnd 4: Sl st to center st of 7-hdc group, ch 1, sc in same st, * ch 6, sk 5 sts, dc in next st, ch 6, sk 5 sts, sc in next st, rep from * 5 times more, sl st to first sc.

Rnd 5: Ch 1, 9 sc in each ch-6 sp around, sl st to first sc.

Rnd 6: Ch 3 for first dc, dc in next st, ch 2, * sk next st, dc in each of next 2 sts, ch 2, rep from * around, sl st to top of beg ch.

Rnd 7: Ch 3 for first dc, * sk next dc, ch-2 sp, and next dc, dc in next dc, ch 6, dc around post of dc just made, ch 3, dc in next dc, rep from * around, sl st to top of beg ch.

Rnd 8: Ch 1, sc in same st, * 7 hdc in next ch-6 sp, 4 sc in next ch-3 sp, rep from * around, sl st to first sc.

Rnd 9: Sc in same st, * ch 6, sk 3 sts, (dc, ch 3, dc) in next st, ch 6, sk 3 sts, sc in next st, ch 3, sk 2 sts, sc in next st, rep from * around, sl st to first sc. Fasten off.

Finishing: Cut 2 (3½″) circles from fabric. Finish as for previous sachet, weaving ribbon through rnd-6 beading sps to join. Tie ribbon in a bow. Trim and knot ribbon ends.

ECRU SACHET

FINISHED SIZE
Approximately 4″ diameter.

MATERIALS
Size 30 crochet thread: 1 (563-yd.) ball ecru.
Size #10 steel crochet hook, or size to obtain gauge.
Scrap of white cotton fabric.
Thread to match.
Small amount of potpourri.
1 yard (⅛″-wide) burgundy satin ribbon.

GAUGE
Motif = 4″ diameter.

DIRECTIONS
Motif (make 2): Ch 8, join with a sl st to form a ring.

Rnd 1: Ch 3 for first dc, 23 dc in ring, sl st to top of beg ch—24 dc counting beg ch.

Rnd 2: Ch 3 for first dc, sk next dc, dc in next dc, ch 8, dc in top of dc just made, * ch 5, yo 3 times, sk next dc, insert hook in next st, yo and draw up a lp, (yo and through 2 lps on hook) twice—3 lps rem on hook, sk next dc, dc in next dc, (yo and through 2 lps on hook) twice, ch 5, dc in top of dc just made, rep from * around, ch 5, sl st to 3rd ch of ch-8.

Rnd 3: Ch 1, 5 sc in each sp around, sl st to first sc—80 sts.

Rnds 4-8: Ch 1, sc in each st around, sl st to first sc.

Rnd 9: Ch 3 for first dc, dc in each st around, sl st to top of beg ch.

Rnd 10: Ch 3 for first dc, sk next dc, dc in next dc, ch 8, dc in top of dc just made, * ch 5, yo 3 times, sk next dc, insert hook in next st, yo and draw up a lp, (yo and through 2 lps on hook) twice—3 lps rem on hook, sk next dc, dc in next dc, (yo and through 2 lps on hook) twice, ch 5, dc in top of dc just made, rep from * around, ch 5, sl st to 3rd ch of ch-8.

Rnd 11: Sl st in next sp, ch 3 for first dc, ch 2, dc in same sp, * ch 3, sc in next sp, ch 3, (dc, ch 2, dc) in next sp, rep from * around, sl st to top of beg ch.

Rnd 12: Sl st in next sp, ch 3 for first dc, ch 2, dc in same sp, * ch 3, sc in next sc, ch 3, (dc, ch 2, dc) in next sp, rep from * around, sl st to top of beg ch. Fasten off.

Finishing: Cut 2 (2½″) circles from fabric. Finish as for first sachet, weaving ribbon through rnd-9 beading sps to join. Tie ribbon in a bow. Trim and knot ribbon ends.

WHITE SACHET

FINISHED SIZE
Approximately 4″ square.

MATERIALS
Size 8 pearl cotton thread: 1 (95-yd.) ball white.
Size #12 steel crochet hook, or size to obtain gauge.
Scrap of white cotton fabric.
Thread to match.
Small amount of potpourri.
1 yard (⅛″-wide) ivory satin ribbon.

GAUGE
Square = 4″.

DIRECTIONS

Square (make 2): Ch 6, join with a sl st to form a ring.

Rnd 1: Ch 2 for first hdc, 15 hdc in ring, sl st to top of beg ch.

Rnd 2: Ch 3 for first hdc and ch 1, (hdc in next st, ch 1) 15 times, sl st to 2nd ch of beg ch.

Rnd 3: Sl st in next sp, sc in same st, * ch 16, sk 4 hdc, sc in next ch-1 sp, rep from * 3 times more, sl st to first sc.

Rnd 4: Ch 1, 16 sc in each ch-16 sp around, sl st to first sc.

Rnd 5: Sc in same st, * (ch 12, sk 3 sts, sc in next st) 3 times, ch 12, sk 4 sts, sc bet next 2 sts, rep from * around, sl st to first sc.

Rnd 6: Sl st in next 4 sts of ch-12 lp, 3 sc in same lp, * ch 6, 3 sc in next ch-12 lp, rep from * around, sl st to first sc.

Rnd 7: Sl st in next 3 sc, sc in same st, * ch 6, (4 dc, ch 3, 4 dc) in next ch-6 sp for corner, (ch 6, sc in next ch-6 sp) 3 times, rep from * around, sl st to first sc.

Rnd 8: Ch 1, 6 sc in next ch-6 sp, * ch 6, 3 hdc in next corner ch-3 sp, ch 6, (6 sc in next ch-6 sp) 4 times, rep from * around, sl st to first sc.

Rnd 9: Ch 4 for first dc and ch 1, (sk next st, dc in next st, ch 1) to corner, * sk 1 hdc, (dc, ch 1, dc) in center hdc of corner, ch 1, sk next hdc, dc in next st, (ch 1, sk next st, dc in next st) to next

corner, ch 1, rep from * around, sl st to 3rd ch of beg ch.

Rnd 10: Sl st in next sp, ch 6 for first dc and ch 3, (sk 2 dc, dc in next sp, ch 3) to sp before corner, dc in sp before corner, * (3 dc, ch 1, 3 dc) in corner sp, sk 1 dc, dc in next sp, (ch 3, sk 2 dc, dc in next sp) to sp before next corner, rep from * around, sl st to 3rd ch of beg ch.

Rnd 11: Ch 6 for first dc and ch 3, * dc in next dc, ch 3, dc in next dc, ch 5, sk 2 dc, dc in each of next 2 dc, (dc, ch 3, dc) in corner sp, dc in each of next 2 dc, ch 5, sk 2 dc, (dc in next dc, ch 3) twice, (dc in next dc, 2 dc in next sp, dc in next dc, ch 3) twice, rep from * around, end with 2 dc in last sp, sl st to 3rd ch of beg ch.

Rnd 12: Ch 1, * (2 sc, ch 3, 2 sc) in each of next 2 sps, (3 sc, ch 3, 3 sc) in next sp, sc in each of next 3 sts, (2 sc, ch 3, 2 sc) in corner sp, sc in each of next 3 sts, (3 sc, ch 3, 3 sc) in next sp, (2 sc, ch 3, 2 sc) in each of next 2 sps, sc in each of next 2 dc, ch 3, sc in each of next 2 dc, (2 sc, ch 3, 2 sc) in next sp, sc in each of next 2 dc, ch 3, sc in each of next 2 dc, rep from * around, sl st to first sc. Fasten off.

Finishing: Cut 2 (3½″) squares from fabric. Finish as for first sachet, weaving ribbon through rnd-9 beading sps to join. Tie ribbon in a bow. Trim and knot ribbon ends.

Heirloom Comforter

Soft down feathers fill this white comforter, subtly accented by large white crocheted squares.

FINISHED SIZE

Duvet: Approximately 56″ x 84″.
Pillow: Approximately 28″ square.

MATERIALS

Size 10 crochet thread: 10 (400-yd.) balls white.
Size #1 steel crochet hook, or size to obtain gauge.
6⅔ yards (60″-wide) white fabric.

Thread to match.
3 king-size goose-down pillows, or stuffing (for duvet).
6½ yards white satin piping (for pillow).
2 (28″-square) pillow forms, or stuffing.

GAUGE

Square = 28″.

DIRECTIONS

Square (make 8): (Ch 3, dc in 3rd ch from hook, ch 3, dc bet prev ch-3 and dc to make a ch-link) 8 times, join with sl st in center of first link to form a ring of ch-links.

Rnd 1: Working along ch side of each link, * ch 3, 2 dc in same link, ch 3, sl st in same link **, ch 6, sl st in next link, rep from * around, end last rep at **, ch 3, dc in base of beg ch.

Rnd 2: Sc in same st, * ch 6, sc bet next 2 dc **, ch 6, sc in next ch-6 lp, rep from * around, end last rep at **, ch 3, dc in first sc.

Rnd 3: * Ch 12, dc in 4th ch from hook, ch 3, sl st in next lp, rep from * around, end with sl st in base of beg ch.

Rnd 4: Sl st in each st to lp above next dc, ch 3, 10 dc in same lp, (ch 3, sc in next lp, ch 3, 11 dc in next lp) 7 times, ch 3, sc in next lp, ch 3, sl st to top of beg ch.

Rnd 5: * Ch 9, sc in 6th st of dc group, ch 9, sc in last st of same dc group **, ch 9, sc in first st of next dc group, rep from * around, end last rep at **, ch 4, dtr in base of beg ch.

Rnd 6: (Ch 10, sc in next lp) around, end with ch 5, dtr in base of beg ch.

Rnd 7: Work * 15 tr in next lp, sc in next lp, (ch 2, tr) 3 times in next sc, ch 2, sc in next lp, rep from * around, sl st to top of first tr.

Rnd 8: * Ch 6, sk 3 tr, sc in next tr, (ch 6, sk 2 tr, sc in next tr) 3 times, ch 6, sk 2 tr, sc in next sc, ch 6, 2 dc in next tr, (ch 2, 2 dc in next tr) twice **, ch 6, sc in next sc, rep from * around, end last rep at **, ch 3, dc in base of beg ch.

Rnd 9: Sc in same st, * (ch 12, sk 2 lps, sc in next lp) twice **, ch 12, sk all 2-dc groups, sc in next lp, rep from * around, end last rep at **, ch 6, yo 5 times, draw up a lp in first sc, (yo and through 2 lps on hook) 6 times (qdtr made).

Rnd 10: Sc in same st, (ch 13, sc in next lp) around, end with ch 7, qdtr in first sc.

Rnd 11: Sc in same st, (ch 14, sc in next lp) around, end with ch 7, yo 6 times, draw up a lp in first sc, (yo and through 2 lps on hook) 7 times.

Rnd 12: Sc in same st, * ch 15, sc in next lp, ch 15, tr in 5th ch from hook, ch 5, sc in same lp as prev sc, ch 15, sc in next lp, (ch 12, sc in next lp) 4 times, rep from * around, sl st to first sc.

Rnd 13: Sl st in next lp, * 8 sc in lp, ch 6, 17 tr in corner lp above rnd 12 tr, ch 6, 8 sc in next lp, (12 sc in next lp) 4 times, rep from * around, sl st to first sc.

Rnd 14: Sc in same st, ch 6, * sk 7 sc, 3 dc in next sc, ch 6, sk 2 tr, sc in next tr, (ch 3, sk 1 tr, sc in next tr) 6 times, ch 6, sk last 2 tr, 3 dc in next sc, ch 6, sk 7 sc, sc in next sc, (ch 6, sk 5 sc, sc in next sc) 8 times, ch 6, rep from * around, sl st in first sc.

Rnd 15: Ch 4 for first tr, keeping last lp of each st on hook, work 2 tr in same st, yo and through all lps on hook (beg cluster completed), * ch 1, 3 dc in next dc, ch 1, sk 1 dc, 3 dc in next dc, ch 6, (sc in next ch-3 lp, ch 3) 3 times, (sc in same lp, ch 3, sc in next lp, ch 3) twice, sc in next lp, ch 6, 3 dc in next dc, ch 1, sk 1 dc, 3 dc in next dc, keeping last lp of each st on hook, work 3 tr in next sc, yo and through all lps on hook (3-tr cluster completed), ch 6, sc in next lp, ch 6, (6 sc in next lp) 6 times, ch 6, sc in next lp, ch 6 **, 3-tr cluster in next sc, rep from * around, end last rep at **, sl st to top of first cluster.

Rnd 16: Ch 10 for first tr and ch 6, * tr in ch-1 sp bet 3-dc groups, ch 6, tr in next lp, (ch 6, sk 1 ch-3 lp, tr in next lp) 4 times, ch 6, tr in ch-1 sp bet 3-dc groups, ch 6, tr in top of cluster, ch 6, sk next lp and next sc, tr in next lp, (ch 6, sk 5 sc, tr in next sc) 5 times, ch 6, tr in next lp, ch 6 **, tr in top of cluster, ch 6, rep from * around, end last rep at **, sl st to 4th ch of beg ch.

Rnd 17: Ch 4 for first tr, tr in same st, [ch 6, keeping last lp of each st on hook, work 2 tr in next tr, yo and through all lps on hook (2-tr cluster completed)] twice, * ch 6, 2-tr cluster in next lp, ch 6, 2-tr cluster in next tr, ch 6, (tr, ch 2) 5 times in next tr for corner, ch 4, 2-tr cluster in next tr, ch 6, 2-tr cluster in next lp **, (ch 6, 2-tr cluster in next tr) 13 times, rep from * around, end last rep at **, (ch 6, 2-tr cluster in next tr) 10 times, ch 6, sl st to top of beg ch.

Rnd 18: Ch 4 for first tr, (5 tr in next lp, tr in next cluster) 4 times, * ch 2, dc in next lp, ch 2, (2 tr in next tr, ch 3) 4 times, 2 tr in next tr, ch 2, dc in next lp, ch 2 **, (tr in next tr, 5 tr in next lp) 16 times, tr in next tr, rep from * around, end last rep at **, (tr in next tr, 5 tr in next lp) 12 times, sl st to top of beg ch.

Rnd 19: Ch 10 for first tr and ch 6, sk 5 tr, tr in next tr, (ch 6, sk 5 tr, tr in next tr) 3 times, * ch 6, sk next dc, (2 tr in next tr, tr in next tr, ch 3) 5 times, ch 3, sk next dc, tr in next tr **, (ch 6, sk 5 tr, tr in next tr) 16 times, rep from * around, end last rep at **, (ch 6, sk 5 tr, tr in next tr) 11 times, ch 6, sl st to 4th ch of beg ch.

Rnd 20: Ch 4 for first tr, (tr, ch 5, 2 tr) in same st (beg shell completed), ch 1, [(2 tr, ch 5, 2 tr) in next tr (shell completed), ch 1] 4 times, * (shell in center st of next 3-tr group, ch 1) 5 times **, (shell in next tr, ch 1) 17 times, rep from * around, end last rep at **, (shell in next tr, ch 1) 12 times, sl st to top of beg ch.

Rnd 21: Sl st to center of next lp, sc in same lp, (ch 9, sc in next lp) around, sl st to first sc.

Rnd 22: Rep rnd 21.

Rnd 23: Ch 9 for first tr and ch 5, tr in same st, [ch 3, (3 tr, ch 3, 3 tr) in center st of next lp (shell completed), ch 3, (tr, ch 5, tr) in center st of next lp] twice, * ch 3, shell in center st of next lp, ch 3, (3 tr, ch 5, 3 tr) in center st of next lp for corner **, [ch 3, shell in center st of next lp, ch 3, (tr, ch 5, tr) in center st of next lp] 10 times, rep from * around, end last rep at **, [ch 3, shell in center st of next lp, ch 3, (tr, ch 5, tr) in center st of next lp] 7 times, ch 3, shell in center st of next lp, ch 3, sl st to 4th ch of beg ch.

Rnd 24: Sl st to center of next lp, sc in same lp, (ch 7, sc in next lp) 5 times, * (ch 10, sc in next lp) twice **, (ch 7, sc in next lp) 20 times, rep from * around, end last rep at **, (ch 7, sc in next lp) 14 times, ch 7, sl st to first sc.

Rnd 25: Sl st to center of next lp, sc in same lp, * (ch 6, sc in next lp) to next corner, ch 3, (3 dc, ch 2, 3 dc) in corner sc, ch 3, sc in next lp, rep from * around, ch 6, sl st to first sc.

Rnd 26: Ch 2 for first hdc, (6 hdc in next lp, hdc in next sc) 5 times, * 3 hdc in next ch-3 lp, hdc in each of next 3 dc, 3 hdc in corner lp, hdc in each of next 3 dc, 3 hdc in next ch-3 lp, hdc in next sc **, (6 hdc in next lp, hdc in next sc) 21 times, rep from * around, end last rep at **, (6 hdc in next lp, hdc in next sc) 16 times, sl st to top of beg ch.

Rnd 27: Ch 1, sc in same st, (ch 10, sk 6 hdc, sc in next hdc) 4 times, * (ch 10, sk 5 hdc, sc in next hdc) 5 times **, (ch 10, sk 6 hdc, sc in next hdc) 19 times, rep from * around, end last rep at **, (ch 10, sk 6 hdc, sc in next hdc) 14 times, ch 10, sl st to first sc.

Rnd 28: Sl st in next lp, ch 3 for first dc, (2 dc, ch 5, 3 dc) in same lp, * (3 dc, ch 5, 3 dc) in next lp, rep from * around, sl st to top of beg ch.

Finishing: *Note:* Use ½″ seam. For duvet, cut 2 (57″ x 85″) pieces of white fabric. With right sides facing, stitch together, leaving a 15″ opening in the center of each seam. Turn and press.

Mark fabric in half lengthwise and then in thirds widthwise, forming 6 (28″-square) pockets. Stitch through both layers along marked lines.

Stuff 1 pocket, using half of the down from 1 pillow. Turn under seam allowance and slipstitch pocket opening closed. Repeat for 5 remaining pockets.

Place a crocheted square right side up on each pocket. Slipstitch along seam lines.

For pillow, cut 2 (29″) squares from fabric. Cut piping in half. With raw edges aligned, stitch 1 half of piping to right side of 1 fabric square, rounding corners. With right sides facing and piping toward center, stitch back to front along 3 sides. Turn and insert pillow form. Turn under seam allowance and slipstitch opening closed.

Place a crocheted square right side up on pillow. Slipstitch to pillow at seam line.

Repeat for 2nd pillow.

Pillow Dressings

Dress up a purchased throw pillow by wrapping it with a crocheted band. Work the squares in a color that coordinates with your decorating scheme.

■ ■ ■

FINISHED SIZE
Approximately 6½″ x 26″.

MATERIALS
Worsted-weight nylon-cotton blend slubbed texture: 2 oz. light green.

Size #2 steel crochet hook, or size to obtain gauge.

16″ x 18″ throw pillow to coordinate with yarn.

1⅝ yards (1/16″-wide) light green satin ribbon.

13½″ square of light green fabric.

Thread to match.

GAUGE
Square = 6½″.

DIRECTIONS
Note: The following directions will make a band for 1 throw pillow.

Square (make 2): Ch 6, join with a sl st to form a ring.

Rnd 1: Ch 3 for first dc, 15 dc in ring, sl st to top of beg ch.

Rnd 2: Ch 4 for first tr, tr in each of next 3 sts, (ch 5 for corner, tr in each of next 4 sts) 3 times, ch 5, sl st to top of beg ch.

Rnd 3: Sl st in next st, sc bet 2nd and 3rd tr of next 4-tr group, ch 4, (13 dc in next ch-5 sp, ch 3, sc bet 2nd and 3rd tr of next 4-tr group, ch 3) 3 times, 13 dc in last ch-5 sp, dc in first sc.

Rnd 4: Sc in sp just made, ch 3, sc in next sp, * (ch 3, sk 1 dc, sc in next dc) 6 times **, (ch 3, sc in next sp) twice, rep from * twice more, end last rep at **, dc in first sc.

Rnd 5: Sc in sp just made, * ch 4, sc in next sp, rep from * around, dc in first sc.

Rnd 6: Sc in sp just made, * ch 5, sc in next sp, rep from * around, ch 2, dc in first sc.

Rnd 7: Sc in sp just made, (ch 5, sc in next sp) 5 times, * ch 3, (3 tr, ch 5, sl st in 5th ch from hook to make a picot, 3 tr) in next sp for corner, ch 3 **, (sc in next sp, ch 5) 6 times, sc in next sp, rep from * twice more, end last rep at **, sc in next sp, ch 5, sl st to first sc. Fasten off.

Assembly: Whipstitch squares tog along 1 edge.

Finishing: Cut ribbon in half. Knot 1 length around 16″ width of pillow at center, pulling ribbon tightly so that width of pillow is now 13″. Repeat with 2nd ribbon. Slide ribbons to center of pillow about 3″ apart.

Fold the fabric square in half with right sides facing. Using ¼″ seam, stitch along all raw edges, leaving a small opening for turning. Turn and slipstitch opening closed. Press. Slipstitch ends of the crocheted piece to ends of the fabric band, forming a tube. Slip tube over pillow, hiding ribbon ties (see photograph).

Best Seat in The House

Crochet small squares, rectangles, and triangles and join them with rounds of single crochet to make this soft chair seat.

FINISHED SIZE
Approximately 19″ square.

MATERIALS
Worsted-weight wool: 4 oz. each blue, green, mauve.
Size G crochet hook, or size to obtain gauge.
1½ yards (45″-wide) blue fabric (to match yarn).
Thread to match.
2⅛ yards (1″) cording.
18″-square pillow form.

GAUGE
Center square = 3″.

DIRECTIONS
Center square: With mauve, ch 6, join with a sl st to form a ring.
Rnd 1: Ch 1, (sc in ring, ch 3) 8 times, sl st to first sc.
Rnd 2: Sl st in next sp, ch 3 for first dc, 2 dc in same sp, * ch 3, dc in next sp, ch 3 **, 3 dc in next sp for corner, rep from * 3 times more, end last rep at **, sl st to top of beg ch.
Rnd 3: Sl st to center st of 3-dc group, ch 3 for first dc, 2 dc in same st, * dc in next dc, (ch 3, dc in next sp) twice, ch 3, dc in next dc **, 3 dc in next dc for corner, rep from * around, end last rep at **, sl st to top of beg ch. Fasten off.
Rnd 4: Join blue in center st of any corner, ch 3 for first dc, 2 dc in same st, * dc in next dc, (ch 2, 2 dc in next sp) 3 times, ch 2, sk 1 dc, dc in next dc **, 3 dc in next dc for corner, rep from * around, end last rep at **, sl st to top of beg ch. Fasten off.
Rnd 5: Join green in center st of any corner, * 3 sc in same st, sc evenly to next corner, rep from * around, sl st to first sc. Fasten off.

Corner triangle: Work a blue triangle on each side of center square.
Row 1: With right side facing, join blue in 3rd sc of any corner, sc to first sc of next corner. Ch 1, turn.
Rows 2-8: Sk first sc, sc in each st across, leave last st unworked. Ch 1, turn.
Row 9: Draw up a lp in each of last 2 sc, yo and through all lps on hook. Fasten off.
Rep rows 1-9 to work triangles on 3 rem sides of square. Join yarn in either the first or last sc of each corner group; do not work in center st of corners.

Border: Join green in any corner, * 3 sc in same st, sc evenly to next corner, rep from * around, sl st to first sc. Fasten off.

Outer triangle: Work a mauve triangle on each side of square according to corner triangle directions above.

Border: Rnd 1: Join green in any corner, * 3 sc in same st, sc evenly to next corner, rep from * around, sl st to first sc. Fasten off.
Rnd 2: Join blue in any corner, * 3 sc in corner, sc evenly to next corner, rep from * around, sl st to first sc.
Rnds 3 and 4: Ch 1, * sc in each sc to corner, 3 sc in corner, rep from * around, sl st to first sc. Fasten off after rnd 4.
Rnd 5: Join mauve in any corner, ch 3 for first dc, 2 dc in same st, * (ch 2, sk next sc, dc in next sc) to next corner, ch 2 **, sk 2 sc, 3 dc in next st for corner, rep from * around, end last rep at **, sl st to top of beg ch.
Rnd 6: Sl st to center st of corner, ch 3 for first dc, 2 dc in same st, * (ch 2, dc in next sp) to corner, ch 2, 3 dc in center dc of corner, rep from * around, sl st to top of beg ch. Fasten off.
Rnd 7: Join green in center st of any corner, * 3 sc in same st, (ch 2, sc in next sp) to next corner, ch 2, rep from * around, sl st to first sc.
Rnd 8: Sl st to center st of corner, ch 3 for first dc, 2 dc in same st, * (ch 2, dc in next sp) to next corner, ch 2, 3 dc in center st of corner, rep from * around, sl st to top of beg ch. Fasten off.

Border square (make 20): With mauve, ch 6, join with a sl st to form a ring.
Rnd 1: Ch 1, 8 sc in ring, sl st to first sc.
Rnd 2: Ch 3 for first dc, 2 dc in same st, * ch 2, dc in next st, ch 2 **, 3 dc in next st, rep from * twice more, end last rep at **, sl st to top of beg ch.

Rnd 3: Ch 3 for first dc, * 3 dc in next dc for corner, dc in next dc, (ch 2, dc in next sp) twice, ch 2, dc in next dc **, rep from * around, end last rep at **, sl st to top of beg ch. Fasten off.

Rnd 4: Join blue in center st of any corner, ch 3 for first dc, 2 dc in same st, * dc in next dc, (ch 1, 2 dc in next sp) 3 times, ch 1, sk 1 dc, dc in next dc **, 3 dc in next dc for corner, dc in next dc, rep from * around, end last rep at **, sl st to top of beg ch. Fasten off.

Assembly: Whipstitch border squares around outside edge of center square (see photograph).

Border: Join green in any corner, * 3 sc in corner, sc evenly to next corner, rep from * around, sl st to first sc. Fasten off.

Finishing: *Note:* Use ½″ seam. Cut 2 (19″) squares from fabric. Cut 2 (2½″ x 36″) strips for ties. Cut 3¼″-wide bias strips, piecing as needed, to measure 2⅛ yards.

To cover cording, place cording in center of wrong side of bias strip. Using a zipper foot and matching raw edges, stitch close to cording. With raw edges aligned, stitch piping to right side of chair seat front, rounding corners slightly. Match and slipstitch ends of piping together.

To make ties, fold 1 (2½″ x 36″) strip lengthwise, right sides facing. Cut ends diagonally to form a point. Using ¼″ seam, stitch along length of strip, leaving a small opening for turning. Turn. Slipstitch opening closed; press. Fold tie in half to form a V. Matching fold of tie to raw edge of chair seat back, baste to right side of fabric, 2½″ from 1 corner. Repeat for 2nd tie at adjacent corner.

Place chair seat front on back, right sides facing, with piping and ties toward center. Stitch 3 sides, securing tie folds in seam. Clip corners and turn. Insert pillow form. Turn under seam allowance and slipstitch opening closed.

Place crocheted square right side up on chair seat front and slipstitch to seam.

Diamonds & Squares

Join diamonds and squares for a sophisticated pair of pillows.

■ ■ ■

COUNTRY COLORS

FINISHED SIZE
Approximately 18″ square.

MATERIALS
Worsted-weight wool-mohair blend: 4 oz. each rust, blue, dark green.

Size G crochet hook, or size to obtain gauge.

1¼ yards (45″-wide) rust fabric.

Thread to match.

2⅛ yards (1″) cording.

18″-square pillow form.

GAUGE
Square = 9″.

DIRECTIONS
Square (make 4): **Row 1:** With rust, ch 5, sc in 2nd ch from hook and each of next 3 ch. Ch 1, turn.

Rows 2 and 3: Sc in each sc across. Ch 1, turn. Fasten off after row 3.

Rnd 1: Join blue in last st of row 3, 3 sc in same st for corner, * sc in each of next 3 sc, 3 sc in next sc for corner, rep from * around, sl st to first sc.

Rnd 2: Sl st in next sc, ch 3 for first dc, 2 dc in same st, * dc evenly to next corner, 3 dc in center st of next corner, rep from * around, sl st to top of beg ch. Fasten off.

Rnd 3: Join dark green in any corner, * 3 sc in same corner, sc evenly to next corner, rep from * around, sl st to first sc. Fasten off.

Rnd 4: Join rust in any corner, ch 3 for first dc, 2 dc in same st, * dc evenly to next corner, 3 dc in next corner, rep from * around, sl st to top of beg ch. Fasten off.

Rnd 5: Join dark green in any corner, * 3 sc in same corner, sc evenly to next corner, rep from * around, sl st to first sc. Fasten off.

Corner triangle: Work a blue triangle on each side of square.

Row 1: With right side facing, join blue in 3rd sc of any corner, sc to first sc of next corner. Ch 1, turn.

Rows 2-6: Sk first sc, sc in each st across, leave last st unworked. Ch 1, turn.

Row 7: Draw up a lp in each of last 2 sc, yo and through all lps on hook. Fasten off.

Rep rows 1-7 to work triangles on 3 rem sides of square. Join yarn in either the first or last sc of each corner group; do not work in center st of corners.

Border: Rnd 1: Join dark green in any corner, * 3 sc in same st, sc evenly to next corner, rep from * around, sl st to first sc. Fasten off.

Rnd 2: Join rust in any corner, working in bk lps only, ch 3 for first dc, 2 dc in same corner, ch 2, * (sk next sc, dc in next sc, ch 2) 9 times, 3 dc in next corner, ch 2, rep from * around, sl st to top of beg ch.

Rnd 3: Sl st in next st, ch 3 for first dc, 2 dc in same corner, sc in next dc, * (sc, dc, sc) in each of next 10 sps, sc in next dc, 3 dc in next dc, sc in next dc, rep from * around, sl st to top of beg ch.

Rnd 4: Sl st in next st, working in bk lps only, ch 3 for first dc, 4 dc in same st, * (ch 2, dc in next dc) 10 times, ch 2, 5 dc in next corner, rep from * around, sl st to top of beg ch.

Rnd 5: Sl st to center st of corner, ch 1, * 3 sc in same corner, ch 2, sk next 2 dc, (2 sc in next sp, ch 2) 11 times, ch 2, sk next 2 dc, rep from * around, sl st to first sc. Fasten off.

Rnd 6: Join blue in any corner, * 3 sc in corner, (ch 2, 2 sc in next sp) to next corner, rep from * around, sl st to first sc.

Rnd 7: Ch 1, * sc evenly to next corner, 3 sc in next corner, rep from * around, sl st to first sc. Fasten off.

Assembly: Pillow top is 4 blocks square. With wrong sides facing and blue, whipstitch squares tog through bk lps only.

Finishing: *Note:* Use ½″ seam. From rust fabric, cut 19″ squares for front and back. Cut 2¾″-wide bias strips, piecing as needed, to measure 2⅛ yards. To cover cording, place cording in center of wrong side of bias strip. Using a zipper foot and matching raw edges, stitch close to cording. Place piping on right side of pillow front, with raw edges aligned. Stitch, rounding corners slightly. Match and slipstitch ends of piping together. With right sides facing, raw edges aligned, and piping toward center, stitch back to front around 3 sides. Turn and insert pillow form. Turn under seam allowance and slipstitch opening closed. Place crocheted square right side up on pillow front and slipstitch to seam.

ALPINE GREENS

FINISHED SIZE
Approximately 16″ square.

MATERIALS
Sportweight wool: 5 oz. each dark green, blue, light green.

Size F crochet hook, or size to obtain gauge.

½ yard (45″-wide) dark green fabric.

16″-square pillow form.

½ yard (45″-wide) light green fabric.

Thread to match.

1¾ yards (1″) cording.

3½ yards (⅛″-wide) blue satin ribbon.

GAUGE
Small square = 3½″.

DIRECTIONS
Small square (make 29): With dark green, ch 6, join with a sl st to form a ring.

Rnd 1: Ch 5 for first dc and ch 2, (dc in ring, ch 2) 7 times, sl st to 3rd ch of beg ch.

Rnd 2: Sl st to next sp, ch 1, sc in same sp, * ch 2, 3 sc in next sp for corner, ch 2 **, sc in next sp, rep from * around, end last rep at **, sl st to first sc. Fasten off.

Rnd 3: Join blue in center st of any 3-sc corner group, * 3 sc in same st for corner, (ch 2, sc in next sp) twice, ch 2, rep from * around, sl st to first sc. Fasten off.

Rnd 4: Join light green in any corner, * 3 sc in corner, (ch 2, sc in next sp) 3 times, ch 2, rep from * around, sl st to first sc. Fasten off.

Corner triangle: To make center square, work a dark green triangle on each side of 1 small square.

Row 1: With right side facing, join dark green in 3rd sc of any corner, sc to first sc of next corner. Ch 1, turn.

Rows 2-5: Sk first sc, sc in each st across, leave last st unworked. Ch 1, turn.

Row 6: Draw up a lp in each of last 2 sc, yo and through all lps on hook. Fasten off.

Rep rows 1-6 to work triangles on 3 rem sides of center square. Join yarn in either the first or last sc of each corner group; do not work in center st of corners.

Border: Rnd 1: Join blue in corner of center square, * 3 sc in same st, sc evenly to next corner, rep from * around, sl st to first sc. Fasten off.

Rnd 2: Join light green in any corner, working in bk lps only, * 3 sc in same st for corner, sc evenly to next corner, rep from * around, sl st to first sc. Fasten off.

Side rectangle: Work a dark green rectangle on each side of center square.

Row 1: Join dark green in center st of any corner, working in bk lps only, sc evenly to next corner st. Ch 1, turn.

Rows 2-11: Rep row 1. Fasten off after row 11.

Rep rows 1-11 to work rectangles on 3 rem sides of square. Always join yarn in center st of corner.

With dark green, whipstitch a small square into each corner opening of center square.

Border: Rnd 1: Join dark green in any corner, working in bk lps only, * 3 sc in same st for corner, sc evenly to next corner, rep from * around, sl st to first sc.

Rnd 2: Ch 1, * sc evenly to corner, 3 sc in corner, rep from * around, sl st to first sc.

Rnd 3: Rep rnd 2. Fasten off.

Rnd 4: Join blue in any corner, * 3 sc in corner, sc evenly to next corner, rep from * around, sl st to first sc.

Rnds 5 and 6: Rep rnd 2. Fasten off after rnd 6.

Rnd 7: Join light green in any corner, * 3 sc in corner, sc evenly to next corner, rep from * around, sl st to first sc.

Rnds 8 and 9: Rep rnd 2. Fasten off after rnd 9.

Assembly: With light green, whipstitch small squares around outside edge of center square (see photograph).

Finishing: *Note:* Use ½″ seam. From dark green fabric, cut 17″ squares for front and back. With right sides facing, stitch front and back together around 3 sides. Turn and insert pillow form. Turn under seam allowance and slipstitch opening closed. Place crocheted piece right side up on pillow and slipstitch to pillow seam.

From light green fabric, cut 2¾″-wide bias strips, piecing as needed, to measure 1¾ yards. To cover cording, fold bias strip with right sides facing and raw edges aligned. Stitch long edge to form a tube. Turn right side out. Using a bodkin or large safety pin, pull cording through tube. Slipstitch piping to edge of pillow at seam. Match and slipstitch ends of piping together.

Thread a needle with ribbon. Beginning at corner, wrap ribbon around piping at 1″ intervals. Knot ends and conceal under piping.

Jewel-Tone Floor Pillow

Alternate bright jewel colors with black for a floor pillow that is at home in many settings. This square is easily stitched in rounds of single and double crochet.

FINISHED SIZE
Approximately 34″ square.

MATERIALS
Worsted-weight brushed acrylic: 4 oz. black; 2 oz. each pink, light green, light blue, purple, dark pink, aqua, medium green, dark blue.
Size I crochet hook, or size to obtain gauge.
3 yards (45″-wide) blue fabric.
Thread to match.
4 yards (1″) cording.
Stuffing.

GAUGE
Square = 34″.

DIRECTIONS
Note: Square is worked with 2 strands of yarn held tog as one. Do not fasten off black at the end of a rnd; drop it to the back of work to be picked up on a later rnd as needed. Fasten off all other colors at the end of the rnd.

Square: With black, ch 6, join with a sl st to form a ring.
Rnd 1: Ch 3 for first dc, 11 dc in ring, sl st to top of beg ch. Do not fasten off.
Rnd 2: Join pink, ch 1, 2 sc in same st, 2 sc in each st around, sl st to first sc—24 sts around. Fasten off pink.
Rnd 3: With black, ch 3 for first dc, dc in same st, (dc in next st, 2 dc in next st) 11 times, dc in last st, sl st to top of beg ch—36 sts around.

Rnd 4: Join light green, ch 1, (sc, ch 2, sc) in same st for corner, * sc in each of next 8 sts, (sc, ch 2, sc) in next st for corner, rep from * around, sl st to first sc. Fasten off light green.
Rnd 5: With black, sl st in next sp, ch 3 for first dc, (dc, ch 2, 2 dc) in same sp for corner, * dc evenly to next corner sp, (2 dc, ch 2, 2 dc) in corner sp, rep from * around, sl st to top of beg ch. Do not fasten off.
Rnd 6: Join light blue, sl st in next sp, * (2 sc, ch 2, 2 sc) in corner sp, sc evenly to next corner, rep from * around, sl st to first sc. Fasten off light blue.
Rnd 7: With black, sl st in next sp, ch 3 for first dc, (dc, ch 2, 2 dc) in same sp, * sk 1 st, dc evenly to st before next corner, sk 1 st, (2 dc, ch 2, 2 dc) in next corner sp, rep from * around, sl st to top of beg ch. Do not fasten off.
Rnds 8-28: Rep rnds 6 and 7 as established. For rep of rnd 6, use colors in the following order: Purple, dark pink, dark blue, medium green, aqua, pink, medium green, light blue, purple, dark pink, dark blue. Use black for each rep of rnd 7.
Rnd 29: With black, rep rnd 7. Fasten off.

Border: Rnd 1: Join black with sl st in any corner, * sc evenly to next corner, 3 sc in corner, rep from * around.
Rnd 2: Rep rnd 1. Fasten off.

Finishing: *Note:* Use ½″ seam. Cut 35″ squares from fabric for front and back. Cut 3¼″-wide bias strips, piecing as needed, to measure 4 yards.
With right sides facing, stitch pillow front and back together, leaving a 12″ opening for turning. Turn and stuff firmly. Turn under seam allowance and slipstitch opening closed. Place crocheted square right side up on pillow and slipstitch to pillow at seam.
To cover cording, fold bias strip with right sides facing and raw edges aligned. Stitch long edge to form a tube. Turn right side out. Using bodkin or large safety pin, pull cording through tube. Slipstitch piping to edge of pillow at seam. Match and slipstitch ends of piping together.

Elegance in Blue

The dramatic contrast of light and dark on this pillow is created by matching the lining of the double ruffle to the crochet thread.

■ ■ ■

FINISHED SIZE
Approximately 16″ square, not including ruffle.

MATERIALS
Size 10 crochet thread: 2 (175-yd.) balls light blue.

Size #7 steel crochet hook, or size to obtain gauge.

2¼ yards (45″-wide) dark blue fabric (for pillow and ruffle).

1¾ yards (45″-wide) light blue fabric (for ruffle lining).

Thread to match.

16″-square pillow form.

GAUGE

Square = 16″.

DIRECTIONS

Square: Ch 12, join with a sl st to form a ring.

Rnd 1: Ch 10 for first dc and ch 7, (4 dc in ring, ch 7) 3 times, 3 dc in ring, sl st to 3rd ch of beg ch.

Rnd 2: Sl st to center of next lp, ch 10 for first dc and ch 7, 4 dc in same lp, * dc in each dc to next corner lp, (4 dc, ch 7, 4 dc) in next lp for corner, rep from * around, end with 3 dc in same lp as beg, sl st to 3rd ch of beg ch.

Rnds 3-5: Rep rnd 2.

Rnd 6: Sl st to center of next lp, ch 11 for first tr and ch 7, tr in same lp, * sk 2 dc, tr in next dc, ch 5, working across in front of tr just made, tr in ch before first dc (cross st made), tr in 4th dc from corner, (ch 6, sk 5 dc, tr in next dc, sk 3 dc, tr in next dc, ch 5, working across in front of tr just made, tr in first sk dc, tr in dc after cross st) twice, ch 6, sk 5 dc, tr in next dc, sk 3 dc, tr in 3rd ch of corner lp, ch 5, working across in front of tr just made, tr in first sk dc **, tr in 4th ch of corner lp, ch 7, tr in same ch of corner lp, rep from * around, end last rep at **, sl st to 4th ch of beg ch.

Rnd 7: Ch 4 for first tr, * (6 tr, ch 7, 6 tr) in corner, tr in next tr, (ch 5, tr in tr after cross st, 5 tr in next sp, tr in tr before next cross st) to next corner, ch 5 **, tr in tr before corner lp, rep from * around, end last rep at **, sl st to top of beg ch.

Rnd 8: Ch 4 for first tr, tr in each of next 6 tr, * ch 5, 7 tr in corner lp, (ch 5, tr in each of next 7 tr) to next corner lp, rep from * around, end last rep with ch 5, sl st to top of beg ch.

Rnd 9: Ch 4 for first tr, sk next 5 tr, tr in last tr of group, ch 5, working across in front of tr just made, tr in first sk tr, * tr in first ch of next sp, ch 5, tr in last ch of same sp, sk 3 tr, tr in next tr (center st of corner 7-tr group), ch 5, working across in front of tr just made, tr in first st of corner group, tr in same center st of corner, ch 7, tr in same center st, sk 3 tr, tr in last st of corner group, ch 5, tr in same center st of corner, (tr in first ch of next sp, ch 5, sk 3 ch, tr in last ch of same sp, sk 6 tr, tr in last tr of group, ch 5, working across in front of tr just made, tr in first tr of group) 5 times, rep from * around, end last rep with tr in first ch of next sp, ch 5, sl st to top of beg ch.

Rnd 10: Ch 1, working in bk lps only, * sc evenly to next corner lp, 2 sc in first ch of corner lp, sc in each of next 5 ch, 2 sc in last ch of corner, rep from * around, sl st to first sc.

Rnd 11: Ch 4 for first tr, tr in each of next 6 sc, ch 9, sk 6 sc, tr in each of next 7 sc, * (ch 9, sk 2 sc, tr in each of next 7 sc) twice, (ch 9, sk 6 sc, tr in each of next 7 sc) to next corner, rep from * around, end with ch 9, sk 6 sc, sl st to top of beg ch.

Rnd 12: Sl st in next st, ch 4 for first tr, tr in each of next 4 tr, * sk last tr of group, ch 5, tr in next ch-9 lp, ch 5, sk 1 tr **, tr in each of next 5 sts, rep from * around, end last rep at **, sl st to top of beg ch.

Rnd 13: Sl st in next st, ch 4 for first tr, tr in each of next 2 tr, * sk last tr of group, ch 5, tr in ch before next tr, ch 2, sk next tr, tr in ch after sk tr, ch 5, sk first tr of next group **, tr in each of next 3 tr, rep from * around, end last rep at **, sl st to top of beg ch.

Rnd 14: Sl st in next st, ch 7 for first tr and ch 3, * tr in next sp, (ch 4, sc in 4th ch from hook to make a picot, tr in next tr) twice, picot, tr in next sp, ch 3 **, sk 1 tr, tr in next tr, ch 3, rep from * around, end last rep at **, sl st to 4th ch of beg ch. Fasten off.

Finishing: *Note:* Use ½″ seam. From dark blue fabric, cut 17″ squares for front and back. Cut 7″-wide bias strips, piecing as needed, to measure 7½ yards. From light blue fabric, cut 7″-wide bias strips, piecing as needed, to measure 7½ yards. Cut each bias strip in half widthwise to make 4 strips of 3¾ yards each.

To make ruffle, place a dark blue and a light blue bias strip together with right sides facing. Stitch along 1 long edge and both ends. Turn right side out. Divide into fourths and mark. Stitch gathering threads along raw edge through both layers. Repeat for remaining bias strips to make 2nd ruffle.

With dark blue fabrics facing, pin 1 bias strip to right side of pillow front, matching raw edges. Match marks to corners and pull gathering stitches to fit pillow front. Baste through all layers. Place remaining strip over first with light blue side of strips facing. Gather as above and baste through all layers.

Pin pillow back to front, with right sides facing and ruffles toward center. Stitch around 3 sides, making sure not to catch ruffles in seam. Trim corners and seams. Turn and insert pillow form. Turn under seam allowance and slipstitch opening closed.

Place crocheted piece right side up on pillow. Tack center picot of each 3-picot group to seam.

Traveler's Tapestry Bag

Choose from a wide assortment of novelty yarns to embellish rich tapestry fabric with spike stitch squares and make this unique traveling bag.

■ ■ ■

FINISHED SIZE
Approximately 25″ x 18″.

MATERIALS
Bulky-weight acrylic blend bouclé: 14 oz. blue-green (A).
Worsted-weight wool thick-and-thin texture: 18 oz. green, beige, and taupe ombre (B).
Size K crochet hook, or size to obtain gauge.
2½ yards (45″-wide) tapestry fabric.
Thread to match.
1 yard (45″-wide) cotton fabric (for lining).
5 yards (⅝″) cording.
21″ heavy-duty zipper.
3 yards (1¼″-wide) leather strap, or webbing.

GAUGE

Square = 7".

DIRECTIONS

Square (make 12): **Rnd 1:** With A, lp yarn around finger once, insert hook through lp, yo and bring up a lp, complete st as sc, work 7 sc in ring, sl st to first sc.

Rnd 2: Ch 1, sc in same st, working in bk lps only, work 2 sc in each st around, sl st to first sc—16 sc.

Rnd 3: Ch 1, working in bk lps only, * 2 sc in next st, sc in next st, rep from * around, sl st to first sc—24 sc.

Rnd 4: Ch 1, working in bk lps only, * 2 sc in next st, sc in next st, rep from * around, sl st to first sc—36 sc. Fasten off.

Rnd 5: Working with 2 strands held tog as one, join B in any st, ch 1, insert hook through center of motif, yo and draw lp up to the height of current rnd, complete st as sc (spike sc completed), * work a spike sc below next st by inserting hook through work bet rnds 2 and 3, work a spike sc below next st by inserting hook through work bet rnds 3 and 4, sc in each of next 4 sts, spike sc below next st bet rnds 3 and 4, spike sc below next st bet rnds 2 and 3, spike sc below next st through center of motif, rep from * around, sl st to first sc.

Rnd 6: Working in bk lps only, sc in each of next 4 sts, work * 3 sc in next st for corner, sc in each of next 8 sts, rep from * around, sl st to first sc. Fasten off.

Rnd 7: Join A in any corner, ch 1, * 3 sc in corner, sc evenly to next corner, rep from * around, sl st to first sc. Fasten off.

Assembly: With wrong sides facing and A, whipstitch 6 squares tog, through bk lps only, to make a piece 3 squares wide and 2 squares long. Rep with rem 6 squares.

Border: With 2 strands held tog as one, join B with sl st in any corner, * 3 sc in corner, sc evenly to next corner, rep from * around, sl st to first sc.
Rep border around other crocheted piece.

Finishing: *Note:* Use ½" seam. Cut 2 (19" x 26") pieces each from tapestry and lining fabrics for front and back. From remaining tapestry, cut 1¾"-wide bias strips, piecing as needed, to measure 5 yards. To cover cording, place cording in center of wrong side of bias strip. Using a zipper foot and matching raw edges, stitch close to cording. Cut piping in half.

On right side of 1 tapestry piece, draw a rectangle by measuring 2" from top edge, 4" from bottom edge, and 3" from side edges. With raw edges of piping toward center of rectangle, stitch piping along this line, rounding corners. Match and slipstitch ends of piping together. Slipstitch crocheted piece, right side up, along piping stitching line. Repeat for other side of bag.

Turn under ½" along top edge of bag front and back. Stitch 1 edge of zipper to top edge of front. Repeat with other edge of zipper and top edge of back.

With right sides facing, raw edges aligned, and zipper open, stitch side and bottom seams of bag. With right sides facing, align side and bottom seams. Stitch across top and bottom corners of bag as shown in Diagram. Make lining in like manner, omitting zipper, and set aside.

For handles, cut leather strap in half. Fold 1 piece at midpoint. Referring to photograph for placement, position strap on bag front, with cut ends at bottom seam. Stitch. (For leather, use heavy-duty sewing machine.) Repeat with bag back for other handle.

With wrong sides facing, insert lining in bag. Slipstitch lining to bag at zipper.

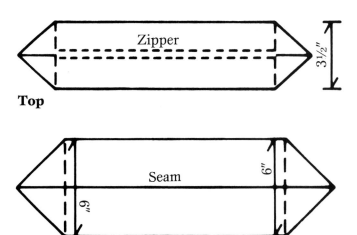

Top

Bottom

Old-Fashioned Throw Rug

Stitch this throw rug from soft cotton fabric strips to add warmth to an entryway. Use either purchased fabric-strip yarn or make your own bias strips.

■ ■ ■

FINISHED SIZE
Approximately 29″ x 38″.

MATERIALS
Bulky-weight cotton fabric bias-cut strips: 8 oz. green; 10 oz. yellow; 16 oz. brown.
Size G crochet hook, or size to obtain gauge.

GAUGE
Square = 7″.

DIRECTIONS
Square (make 9 brown and 3 green): Ch 8, join with a sl st to form a ring.

Rnd 1: Ch 4 for first dc and ch 1, (dc in ring, ch 1) 15 times, sl st to 3rd ch of beg ch.

Rnd 2: Sl st in next sp, ch 3 for first dc, dc in same sp, * dc in next dc, 2 dc in next sp, ch 1 **, 2 dc in next sp, rep from * around, end last rep at **, sl st to top of beg ch.

Rnd 3: Sl st in next dc, ch 3 for first dc, dc in each of next 2 dc, * sk next dc and ch-1 sp, tr in next st, ch 3, tr in sk dc (cross st completed) **, dc in each of next 3 sts, rep from * around, end last rep at **, sl st to top of beg ch.

Rnd 4: Ch 3 for first dc, dc in each of next 2 dc, * 2 dc in sp before cross st, (dc, ch 1, dc) in ch-3 sp of cross st, 2 dc in sp after cross st **, dc in each of next 3 dc, rep from * around, end last rep at **, sl st to top of beg ch.

Rnd 5: Ch 1, sc in same st, * sc in each of next 11 dc, * hdc in next st, dc in next st, tr in next st, 5 tr in ch-1 sp for corner, tr in next st, dc in next st, hdc in next st **, sc in each of next 12 sc, rep from * around, end last rep at **, sl st to top of beg ch. Fasten off.

Border: Rnd 1: Join yellow with sl st in any corner, * 3 sc in corner, sc evenly to next corner, rep from * around, sl st to first sc.

Rnd 2: Rep rnd 1. Fasten off.

Assembly: Rug is 3 squares wide and 4 squares long. Holding 2 squares with wrong sides facing and working through both pieces, join yellow with sl st in any corner, * ch 1, sk next st, sl st in next st, rep from * to next corner. Fasten off. Rep to join squares in 3 strips of 4 each. Rep to join strips in same manner.

Border: Rnd 1: Join yellow in any corner, * (sc, ch 1, sc) in corner, sc evenly to next corner, rep from * around, sl st to first sc. Fasten off.

Rnd 2: Join brown and rep rnd 1. Fasten off.

Rnds 3-7: Working in bk lps only, join green in any corner, * (sc, ch 1, sc) in corner, sc evenly to next corner, rep from * around, sl st to first sc. Fasten off.

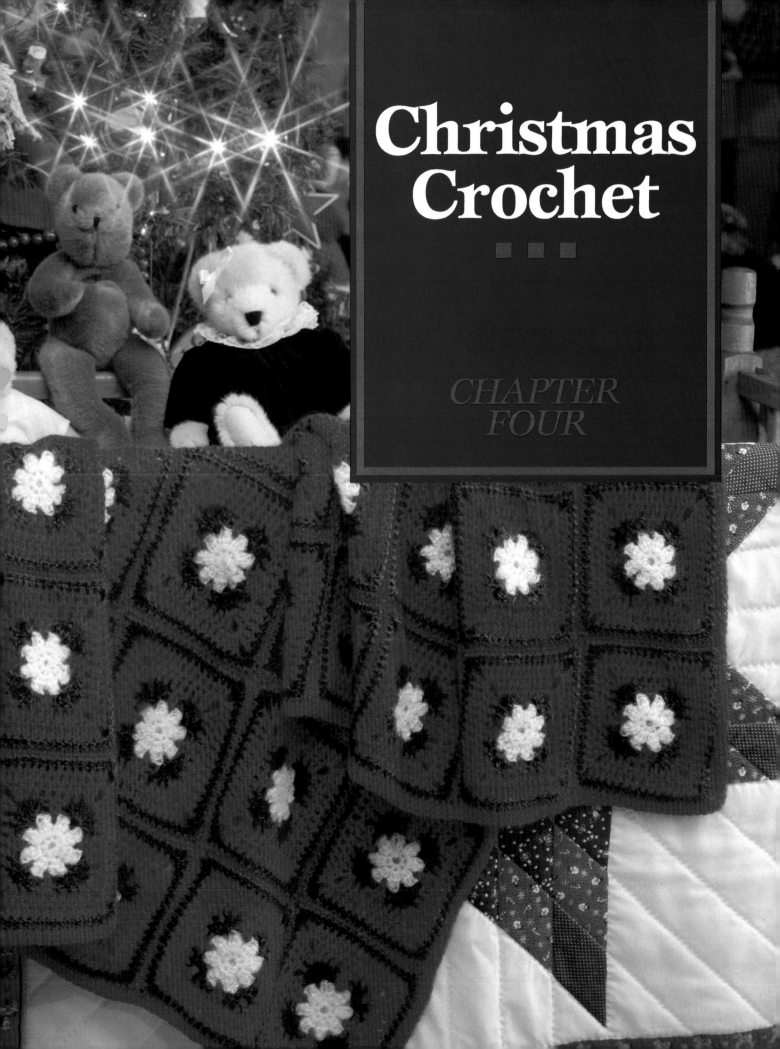

Christmas Crochet

CHAPTER FOUR

The Night Before Christmas

White roses surrounded by bright red and green provide snuggly warmth for Christmas Eve.

■ ■ ■

FINISHED SIZE
Approximately 43″ x 55″.

MATERIALS
Worsted-weight acrylic-mohair blend: 6 oz. white; 13 oz. green; 16 oz. red.
Size H crochet hook, or size to obtain gauge.

GAUGE
Square = 6″.

DIRECTIONS
Note: On rnd 3, carry color not in use along top of prev rnd, working over it with the next group of sts. To avoid holes when changing colors, bring up new color from under dropped color. Always bring up new color as last yo of old color.

Square (make 63): With white, ch 4, join with a sl st to form a ring.

Rnd 1: Ch 1, work 8 sc in ring, sl st to first sc.

Rnd 2: Ch 3 for first dc, keeping last lp of each st on hook, work 2 dc in same st, yo and through all lps on hook (beg cluster completed), [ch 2, keeping last lp of each st on hook, work 3 dc in next st, yo and through all lps on hook (cluster completed)] 7 times, ch 2, sl st to top of first cluster. Fasten off.

Rnd 3: Join green in any ch-2 sp, ch 3 for first dc, (dc, ch 2, 2 dc) in same sp, * change to red with last yo and work 2 dc in next sp, change to green with last yo and work (2 dc, ch 2, 2 dc) in next ch-2 sp for corner, rep from * twice more, end with 2 red dc in last ch-2 sp, sl st to top of beg ch. Fasten off green.

Rnd 4: With red, ch 3 for first dc, dc in each st to corner, * (2 dc, ch 2, 2 dc) in corner ch-2 sp, dc evenly to next corner, rep from * around, sl st to top of beg ch.

Rnd 5: Rep rnd 4. Fasten off.

Rnd 6: Join green in any corner, ch 1, * (2 sc, ch 2, 2 sc) in corner, sc evenly to next corner, rep from * around, sl st to first sc. Fasten off.

Rnd 7: Join red in any corner, ch 1, * 2 sc in corner, sc evenly to next corner, rep from * around, sl st to first sc. Fasten off.

Assembly: Afghan is 7 squares wide and 9 squares long. Whipstitch squares tog with red.

Border: Rnds 1 and 2: Join red with sl st in any corner, ch 1, * 3 sc in corner, sc evenly to next corner, rep from * around, sl st to first sc. Fasten off after rnd 2.

White Christmas Ensemble

Satin fabric and white-and-gold squares become an elegant tree skirt. Complete the ensemble with easy-to-stitch ornaments to decorate your tree and to use as package toppers.

■ ■ ■

FINISHED SIZE
Tree skirt: Approximately 57″ diameter.
Spiral ornament: Approximately 3″ diameter.
Flower ornament: Approximately 3″ diameter.

MATERIALS
Size 5 pearl cotton thread: 8 (53-yd.) balls white.
Fingering-weight flexible metallic: 2 (163-yd.) balls gold metallic.
Size #7 steel crochet hook, or size to obtain gauge.
3½ yards (45″-wide) white satin fabric (for tree skirt).
3½ yards (45″-wide) white fabric for lining (for tree skirt).
Thread to match.
Size 30 crochet thread: 1 (216-yd.) ball white.
1 spool gold metallic thread.
Size #12 steel crochet hook.
Boilable starch.

GAUGE
Tree skirt square = 8½".

DIRECTIONS
Tree skirt square (make 6): For each square, make 8 sections, alternating white and gold. Use size 5 thread, fingering-weight metallic yarn, and size #7 steel hook.

First section: With white, ch 12, join with a sl st to form a ring.

Row 1 (right side): Ch 4 for first tr, (tr in ring, ch 6, dc in top of tr just made, tr in ring) 3 times, tr in ring, ch 2, 10 tr in ring. Turn.

Row 2 (wrong side): Ch 5, sl st in 5th ch from hook to make a picot, sk first tr, sc in each of next 9 tr. Join gold, fasten off white. Turn.

2nd section: Ch 1, sc in same st, ch 3, sk 3 sc on prev section, sc in next sc, ch 9, turn, join with sl st to first sc to form a ring. Turn.

Row 1: Rep row 1 of first section.

Row 2: Ch 2, sc in picot of prev section, ch 3, sl st in 3rd ch from hook to make a picot, sk first tr, sc in each of next 9 tr. Join next color, fasten off prev color. Turn.

Sections 3-7: Rep 2nd section 5 times more, alternating white and gold.

8th section: With gold, work as for 2nd section to end of row 1.

Row 2: Ch 2, sc in picot of prev section, ch 1, sc in picot of first section, ch 2, sl st in 2nd ch from hook to make a picot, sk first tr, sc in each of next 5 tr, sl st to first section, sc in each of next 4 tr, sl st to first section. Fasten off.

Center ring: Join gold in sc of first section in center of motif, ch 1, sc in same st, (sc in next picot, sc in side of next sc) 7 times, sc in last picot, sl st to first sc. Fasten off.

Border: Rnd 1: Join white in center ch-6 lp on first section, ch 10 for first dtr and ch 5, dtr in same lp, * ch 5, tr in next ch-6 lp, ch 5, dc in next lp, ch 5, sc in next lp, ch 5, dc in next lp, ch 5, tr in next lp, ch 5, (dtr, ch 5, dtr) in next lp, rep from * around, sl st to 5th ch of beg ch.

Rnd 2: Sl st in ch-5 sp, ch 2 for first hdc, (2 hdc, ch 3, 3 hdc) in same sp for corner, * 7 hdc in each of next 6 ch-5 sps, (3 hdc, ch 3, 3 hdc) in next corner sp, rep from * around, sl st to top of beg ch.

Rnd 3: Sl st in ch-3 sp, ch 3 for first dc, (dc, ch 4, 2 dc) in same corner, * sk 3 hdc, (2 dc, ch 2, 2 dc) bet next 2 hdc, sk 7 hdc, rep from * 6 times more, sk 3 hdc, (2 dc, ch 4, 2 dc) in corner ch-3 sp, rep from * around, sl st to top of beg ch.

Rnd 4: Sl st in ch-4 sp, ch 4 for first tr, (tr, ch 5, 2 tr) in same corner, * (ch 5, tr in next ch-2 sp) to next corner, ch 5, (2 tr, ch 5, 2 tr) in corner, rep from * around, sl st to top of beg ch.

Rnd 5: Sl st in ch-5 corner sp, ch 4 for first tr, (tr, ch 5, 2 tr) in same corner, * ch 2, sk 1 tr, tr in next tr, (ch 5, tr in next tr) 8 times, ch 2, sk 1 tr, (2 tr, ch 5, 2 tr) in corner, rep from * around, sl st to top of beg ch. Fasten off.

Rnd 6: Join gold in any corner, sc in same corner, ch 4, sc in same corner, * ch 4, sk 1 tr, sc in next tr, (ch 4, sc in next tr, ch 4, sc in next lp) 8 times, (ch 4, sc in next tr) twice, ch 4, sk 1 tr, (sc, ch 4, sc) in corner, rep from * around, sl st to first sc. Fasten off.

Finishing: *Note:* Use ½" seam. Following diagram, make patterns for panels A and B. Transfer markings. Cut 6 panels A and 6 panels B each from satin and from lining fabrics.

With right sides facing and raw edges aligned, stitch 12 satin panels together along long edges, alternating A and B. Do not join last 2 panels; leave open to fit around tree trunk. Repeat with lining panels. With right sides facing, stitch skirt top to lining around all edges, leaving an opening for turning. Clip corners, turn, and slipstitch opening closed.

Tack crochet blocks, right sides up, to lower edges of B panels, aligning points.

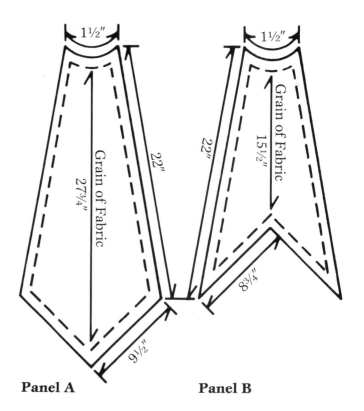

Panel A   **Panel B**

Flower ornament: Use size 30 thread, gold metallic thread, and size #12 steel hook.

With white, ch 6, join with a sl st to form a ring.

Rnd 1: Ch 1, 8 sc in ring, sl st to first sc.

Rnd 2: Ch 1, 2 sc in same st, 2 sc in each st around, sl st to first sc — 16 sts.

Rnd 3: Ch 1, 2 sc in same st, (sc in next st, 2 sc in next st) around, sl st to first sc — 24 sts.

Rnd 4: Ch 1, sc in same st, sc in next st, (2 sc in next st, sc in each of next 2 sts) around, sl st to first sc — 32 sts. Drop white thread but do not fasten off.

Rnd 5: Working with 2 strands of gold thread held tog as one, join with sl st, sc in same st, * insert hook in center of ring, draw up a lp and complete st as sc (spike sc completed), work a spike sc in next st 2 rnds below, sc in next st, spike sc in next st 2 rnds below, sk next st, rep from * 5 times more, sk last st, sl st to first sc — 24 sts. Fasten off gold thread.

Rnd 6: Pick up white thread, ch 2, (2 hdc in next st, hdc in next st) around, sl st to top of beg ch — 36 sts.

Rnd 7: (Ch 9, sk 1 st, sc in next st) around, sl st to base of beg ch.

Rnd 8: Ch 1, (6 sc in next sp, ch 3, 6 sc in next sp) around, sl st to first sc.

Rnd 9: Ch 16 for first tr and ch 11, * (sk next 6-sc group, ch-3 sp, and 6-sc group), tr in st bet sk group and next 6-sc group, ch 11, rep from * around, sl st to 4th ch of beg ch — 9 ch-11 sps.

Rnd 10: Join 1 strand of gold and work with gold and white threads held tog as one, sl st in next sp, ch 3 for first dc, 14 dc in same sp, * ch 2, 15 dc in next sp, rep from * around, ch 2, sl st to top of beg ch.

Finishing: Finish as for Spiral ornament.

Spiral ornament: With size 30 thread, gold metallic thread, and size #12 steel hook, rep directions for tree skirt square except do not work border around spiral motif. Alternate sections, using 1 strand of white thread, and 1 strand each of white and gold metallic threads held tog as one.

Finishing: Prepare starch according to package directions. Soak crocheted piece in starch solution for several minutes. Remove and gently squeeze out excess. Lay piece right side up on an old towel covered with plastic wrap. Beginning at center, stretch piece out to shape and pin, making sure loops are open and points are straight. Let dry completely. Add a length of gold metallic thread for a hanger.

SPIRAL

FLOWER

Baby's First Christmas

Change the ribbon in this throw to match the occasion.

FINISHED SIZE
Approximately 35" x 52".

MATERIALS
Worsted-weight cotton-linen blend thick-and-thin texture: 55 oz. white.
22 yards (⅜"-wide) grosgrain ribbon.
Size G crochet hook, or size to obtain gauge.

GAUGE
Square A = 5".

DIRECTIONS
Square A (make 20): Ch 6, join with a sl st to form a ring.

Rnd 1: Ch 3 for first dc, 2 dc in ring, (ch 2 for corner, 3 dc in ring) 3 times, ch 2 for corner, sl st to top of beg ch.

Rnd 2: Sl st in next sp, ch 3 for first dc, (2 dc, ch 2, 3 dc) in same corner, ch 1, * (3 dc, ch 2, 3 dc) in next sp, ch 1, rep from * twice more, sl st to top of beg ch.

Rnd 3: Sl st in next sp, ch 3 for first dc, (2 dc, ch 2, 3 dc) in same corner, * ch 1, 3 dc in next sp, ch 1, (3 dc, ch 2, 3 dc) in corner, rep from * twice more, ch 1, 3 dc in sp, ch 1, sl st to top of beg ch.

Rnd 4: Sl st in next sp, ch 3 for first dc, (2 dc, ch 2, 3 dc) in same corner, * (ch 1, 3 dc in next sp) twice, ch 1, (3 dc, ch 2, 3 dc) in corner, rep from * twice more, (ch 1, 3 dc in next sp) twice, ch 1, sl st to top of beg ch.

Rnd 5: Sl st in next sp, ch 3 for first dc, (2 dc, ch 2, 3 dc) in same corner, * (ch 1, 3 dc in next sp) 3 times, ch 1, (3 dc, ch 2, 3 dc) in next corner, rep from * twice more, (ch 1, 3 dc in next sp) 3 times, ch 1, sl st to top of beg ch.

Rnd 6: Sl st in next sp, ch 2, (yo and draw up a lp) 4 times in same st, yo and through all lps on hook (puff st completed), ch 3, puff st in same corner, * (ch 1, puff st in center st of next 3-dc group, ch 1, puff st in next sp) to corner, ch 1, (puff st, ch 3, puff st) in corner, rep from * around, sl st to top of first puff st. Fasten off.

Square B (make 18): Rep rnds 1-5 above. Fasten off after rnd 5.

Half square A (make 8): Ch 4, join with a sl st to form a ring.

Row 1: Ch 3 for first dc, 2 dc in ring, ch 2, 3 dc in ring. Turn.

Row 2: Ch 3 for first dc, 2 dc in same st, ch 1, (3 dc, ch 2, 3 dc) in corner ch-2 sp, ch 1, 3 dc in last st. Turn.

Row 3: Ch 3 for first dc, 2 dc in same st, ch 1, 3 dc in next ch-1 sp, ch 1, (3 dc, ch 2, 3 dc) in corner, ch 1, 3 dc in next ch-1 sp, ch 1, 3 dc in last dc. Turn.

Row 4: Ch 3 for first dc, 2 dc in same st, (ch 1, 3 dc in next sp) twice, ch 1, (3 dc, ch 2, 3 dc) in corner, (ch 1, 3 dc in next sp) twice, ch ·1, 3 dc in last dc. Turn.

Row 5: Ch 3 for first dc, 2 dc in same dc, (ch 1, 3 dc in next sp) 3 times, ch 1, (3 dc, ch 2, 3 dc) in corner, (ch 1, 3 dc in next sp) 3 times, ch 1, 3 dc in last dc. Turn.

Row 6: Ch 2, (yo and draw up a lp) 4 times in same st, yo and through all lps on hook (puff st completed), [ch 1, puff st in center dc of next 3-dc group, ch 1, puff st in next ch-1 sp] to corner, ch 1, (puff st, ch 1, puff st) in corner, rep bet [ ] to last st, puff st in last st. Fasten off.

Half square B (make 12): Rep rows 1-5 above. Fasten off after row 5.

Assembly: Following diagram for placement, whipstitch squares tog.

Border: Rnd 1: Join yarn in any corner, ch 1, * (sc, ch 1, sc) in corner, sc evenly to next corner, rep from * around, sl st to first sc.

Rnd 2: Rep rnd 1.

Rnd 3: * Ch 3, 3 dc in next st, sk 3 sts, sl st in next st, rep from * around, sl st to base of beg ch. Fasten off.

Finishing: Cut 1 (9-yard) length of ribbon. Beg in center of long edge of afghan, weave through sps around outer edge of puff sts. Cut 10 (45") lengths of ribbon and weave through sps on inner edge of puff sts (see photograph). Tie ends of ribbons in bows.

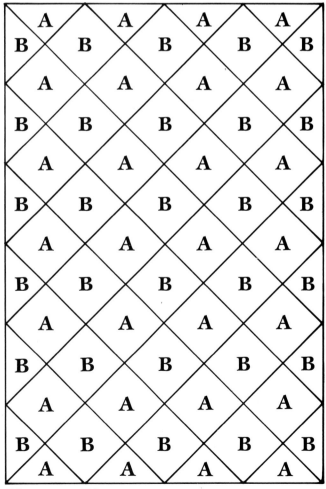

Placement Diagram

A Festive Touch

Wreaths of picot stitches worked in light green thread make a festive but subtle accent for this bolster pillow.

■ ■ ■

FINISHED SIZE
Approximately 7″ x 18″.

MATERIALS
Size 30 crochet thread: 3 (563-yd.) balls light green.
Size #10 steel crochet hook, or size to obtain gauge.
1½ yards (45″-wide) cream print fabric.
Thread to match.
1½ yards (½″) cording.
2 (1½″) button forms to cover.
7″ x 18″ bolster pillow form, or stuffing.

GAUGE

Square = 6".

DIRECTIONS

Square (make 4): *Note:* Ch as specified and sl st in 5th ch from hook to make each picot. Work with fairly tight tension, but be careful to keep work from twisting.

Outer banding (make 2 for each square): **Row 1:** (Ch 6, picot) twice, ch 9, picot, ch 6, picot, ch 2, sc in first ch of row, * (ch 6, picot) twice, (ch 9, picot, ch 6, picot) 3 times, ch 2, sc in center ch bet 4th and 5th picots from hook, rep from * 3 times more—five 4-picot lps. Do not turn.

Row 2: * (Ch 6, picot) twice, ch 2, sc in center ch bet 2nd and 3rd picots of next 4 picots bet 4-picot lps of row 1, (ch 6, picot) twice, ch 2, sc in sc of next 4-picot lp of row 1, rep from * 3 times more. Fasten off.

Row 3: With right side facing and 4-picot lps of row 1 on top, join thread in center ch of last 4-picot lp of row 1. *Note:* Keep picots pointing toward center of each wreath and be careful not to twist work. * (Ch 6, picot) twice, ch 9, picot, ch 6, picot, ch 2, sl st in center ch of next 4-picot lp of row 1, rep from * 3 times more. Do not turn.

Row 4: * (Ch 6, picot) twice, ch 2, sc in center ch bet 2nd and 3rd picots of next 4 picots of row 3, (ch 6, picot) twice, ch 2, sc in same st as sl st of prev row, rep from * 3 times more. Fasten off. Do not turn.

Row 5 (heading row): With right side facing, join thread in sc bet 2nd and 3rd picots of prev row, ch 17 for first dc and ch 14, * sk next 4-picot lp, 1 sc, and 4-picot lp, dc in next sc, rep from * twice more. Fasten off.

Center banding (make 1 for each square): **Row 1:** Rep row 1 of outer banding.

Row 2 (joining row): * (Ch 6, picot) twice, ch 2, sc in center ch bet 2nd and 3rd picots of next 4 picots bet 4-picot lps of row 1, hold an outer banding in back of center banding with heading row at top and wrong sides facing, dc in first dc of heading row on outer banding, (ch 6, picot) twice, ch 2, sc in sc of next 4-picot lp of row 1 on center banding, rep from * 3 times more. Fasten off.

Row 3: Rep row 3 of outer banding.

Row 4: Rep row 2 of center banding with rem outer banding.

Edging: Rnd 1: With right side facing and bandings vertical, join thread with sl st in sc at upper right-hand corner. Ch 4 for first tr, (2 tr, ch 8, 3 tr) in same st for corner, * [ch 8, dc in sc bet next two 4-picot lps, (ch 8, tr in sc bet next two 4-picot lps where heading row is joined) twice, ch 8, dc in sc bet next two 4-picot lps] twice, ch 8, (3 tr, ch 8, 3 tr) in next sc for corner shell, ch 8, dc in sc bet next two 4-picot lps, (ch 8, tr in sc bet next two 4-picot lps, ch 8, dc in sc bet next two 4-picot lps) 3 times, ch 8, corner shell in corner sc, rep from * once more, sl st to top of beg ch.

Rnd 2: Sl st in corner lp, * 7 sc in corner lp, ch 6, sc in next lp, [(ch 6, dc in next lp) 3 times, ch 6, sc in next lp] twice, ch 6, 7 sc in corner lp, (ch 6, sc in next lp) to next corner, rep from * around, sl st to first sc.

Rnd 3: Ch 1, * (sc in each of next 3 sc, 3 sc in next sc, sc in each of next 3 sc) for corner, (5 sc in next lp, sc in next st) to next corner, rep from * around, sl st to first sc. Fasten off.

Assembly: With wrong sides facing, whipstitch squares tog to make a row of 4.

Finishing: *Note:* Use ½" seam. From fabric, cut 1 (19" x 25") rectangle for cover, and 2 (4½" x 25") strips for ends. Cut 1½"-wide bias strips, piecing as needed, to measure 1½ yards. To cover cording, place cording in center of wrong side of bias strip. Using a zipper foot and matching raw edges, stitch close to cording. Cut piping in half and set aside. Fold 1 (4½" x 25") fabric strip with short ends together and right sides facing. Stitch short ends together. Press seam open. Sew gathering stitches along 1 long edge. Do not pull gathering thread. Repeat with remaining fabric strip. Cover buttons with fabric. Set aside.

Fold rectangle with 19" edges together, right sides facing. Stitch together to form a tube. Press seam open. Pin 1 piece of piping around inside of 1 end of tube, right sides facing, raw edges aligned, and piping toward tube center. Stitch. Match and slipstitch ends of piping together. Repeat for other end of tube. With right sides facing and piping still toward center of tube, pin ungathered side of 1 fabric strip inside tube. Matching seams and raw edges, stitch along piping seam. Trim seam. Repeat for other end. Turn bolster cover right side out. Pull gathering stitches on 1 end to fit. Tack gathers securely in place. Insert pillow form. Gather other end to fit as above. Sew a button to center of each end (see photograph).

Wrap row of crocheted squares around pillow next to piping (see photograph). Slipstitch first and last squares together.

A Whisper of Gold

Just a hint of gold at the center of each square lends a luxurious air to this holiday afghan.

■ ■ ■

FINISHED SIZE
Approximately 50″ x 67″, not including fringe.

MATERIALS
Fingering-weight flexible metallic: 10 oz. gold.
Bulky-weight mohair-blend with metallic twist: 14 oz. multicolor gray, purple, bronze, and gold metallic.
Worsted-weight wool-blend: 18 oz. light salmon; 9 oz. medium salmon; 41 oz. dark gray.
Size G crochet hook, or size to obtain gauge.
1 spool gold metallic thread.
Worsted-weight wool-blend: 4 oz. gray tweed.
Size 3 pearl cotton thread: 8 (17-yd.) skeins dark pink; 5 (17-yd.) skeins light pink.
Worsted-weight mohair-blend: 3 oz. light gray.
34 yards (¼″-wide) black and gold ribbon.
34 yards pink tubular satin ribbon.

GAUGE
Square = 5½″.

DIRECTIONS
Square (make 88): With gold metallic, ch 4, join with a sl st to form a ring.

Rnd 1: Ch 3 for first dc, 2 dc in ring, work (ch 2, 3 dc in ring) 3 times, ch 2, sl st to top of beg ch. Fasten off.

Rnd 2: Join light salmon in dc before any ch-2 sp, ch 3 for first dc, * (2 dc, ch 2, 2 dc) in ch-2 sp for corner, dc in next dc, yo twice, insert hook from in front and from right to left around post of next dc, complete st as tr (1 tr/raised front completed), dc in next dc, rep from * around, sl st to top of beg ch. Fasten off.

Rnd 3: Join multicolor yarn in st before any corner sp, ch 3 for first dc, * (2 dc, ch 2, 2 dc) in corner sp, dc in next st, (1 tr/rf around post of next

st, dc in next st) to next corner, rep from * around, sl st to top of beg ch. Fasten off.

Rnd 4: Join dark salmon in st before any corner sp, rep rnd 3. Fasten off.

Rnd 5: Join dark gray in st before any corner sp, ch 3 for first dc, * (2 dc, ch 2, 2 dc) in corner sp, dc in each st to corner, rep from * around, sl st to top of beg ch. Fasten off.

Assembly: Afghan is 8 squares wide and 11 squares long. Thread needle with 1 strand of dark gray and 2 strands of gold thread, and whipstitch squares tog through bk lps only.

Edging: Rnd 1: With 1 strand of dark gray and 1 strand of gold thread held tog as one, join with sl st in any corner, sc in corner, * ch 7, sc in next st, (ch 7, sk 2 sts, sc in next st) to st before next corner, ch 7, sc in st before corner sp **, ch 7, sc in corner sp, rep from * around, end last rep at **, ch 4, tr in first sc. Fasten off gold thread.

Rnd 2: With 1 strand of dark gray, ch 1, sc in same lp, ch 2, * sc in next lp, ch 2, rep from * around, sl st to first sc.

Rnd 3: Ch 1, sc in same st, 2 sc in next ch-2 sp, * sc in next sc, 2 sc in next ch-2 sp, rep from * around, sl st to first sc.

Rnd 4: Ch 3 for first dc, (dc, ch 2, 2 dc) in same st, ch 1, sk 2 sts, * keeping last lp of each st on hook, work 3 dc in same st, yo and through all lps on hook (cluster completed), ch 1, sk 2 sts, (2 dc, ch 2, 2 dc) in next st (shell completed), ch 1, sk 2 sts, rep from * around, sl st to top of beg ch.

Rnd 5: Sl st in next sp, ch 3 for first dc, (dc, ch 2, 2 dc) in same sp, * ch 1, cluster around front post of next cluster, ch 1, shell in ch-2 sp of next shell, rep from * around, sl st to top of beg ch.

Rnd 6: Rep rnd 5. Fasten off.

Fringe: For each tassel, cut 18 (17″) strands as follows: 1 strand gold metallic, 1 strand multicolor yarn, 4 strands light salmon, 2 strands dark gray, 2 strands gray tweed, 2 strands light gray, 2 strands dark pink pearl cotton, 1 strand light pink pearl cotton, 1 strand light gray, 1 strand black and gold ribbon, and 1 strand pink ribbon. Knot a tassel in the ch-2 sp of each shell around afghan.

Christmas Blocks

Use soft-sculpture blocks to spell out a seasonal sentiment.

■ ■ ■

FINISHED SIZE
Each block is approximately 3¼″.

MATERIALS
Size 3 pearl cotton thread: 14 (17-yd.) skeins white; 3 (17-yd.) skeins red.
Size E afghan hook (10″ long), or size to obtain gauge.
Size E crochet hook.
1 yard (45″-wide) red polished cotton fabric.
Thread to match.
Stuffing.

GAUGE
Square = 3¼″.

DIRECTIONS
Afghan st square (make 14): With white and afghan hook, ch 16.
Row 1: *Step 1:* Keeping all lps on hook, draw up a lp through top lp only, in 2nd ch from hook and each ch across—16 lps. Do not turn.
Step 2: Yo and through first lp on hook, * yo and through 2 lps on hook, rep from * across (1 lp rem on hook for first lp of next row). Do not turn.
Row 2: *Step 1:* Keeping all lps on hook, draw up a lp from under 2nd vertical bar, * draw up a lp from under next vertical bar, rep from * across. Do not turn.
Step 2: Rep step 2 of row 1.
Rep both steps of row 2 for 15 rows. Fasten off after last row by working a sl st in each bar across.

Border: With crochet hook, join white with sl st in any corner, ch 1, (sc, ch 1, sc) in same corner, * sc evenly to next corner, work (sc, ch 1, sc) in next corner, rep from * around, sl st to first sc. Fasten off.

Cross-stitch: Following the graphs, work cross-stitch letters on squares with red thread.

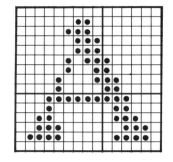

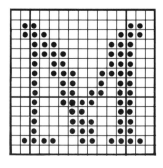

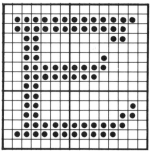

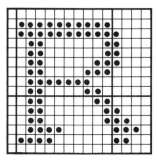

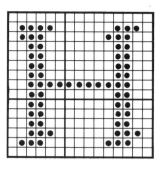

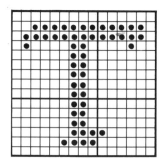

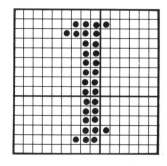

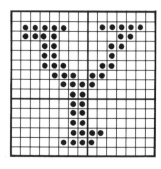

Finishing: *Note:* Use ¼″ seam. For each block, cut 6 (3¾″) squares from fabric. With right sides facing, machine-stitch 4 squares together to make a 13½″ strip. Place ends of strip with right sides together and machine-stitch to make a tube. With right sides facing, machine-stitch the 5th square to 1 open end of tube, matching corners and raw edges. With right sides facing, stitch 3 sides of 6th square to box. Turn and stuff firmly. Turn under seam allowance and slipstitch opening closed. Slipstitch a crocheted and cross-stitched square to 1 side of block. Repeat for remaining blocks.

Leaves of Green

Bright green mercerized thread and tiny popcorn stitches are the base for this simple round motif. When the motifs are joined, the triangular sections resemble poinsettia leaves.

■ ■ ■

FINISHED SIZE
Approximately 16″ diameter.

MATERIALS
Size 8 pearl cotton thread: 5 (95-yd.) balls emerald green.
Size #10 steel crochet hook, or size to obtain gauge.
½ yard (45″-wide) red fabric.
Thread to match.
16″-diameter pillow form.
1⅓ yards red and green beaded trim.

GAUGE
Motif = 3″ diameter.

DIRECTIONS
Motif (make 19): Ch 6, join with a sl st to form a ring.

Rnd 1: Ch 3 for first dc, 17 dc in ring, sl st to top of beg ch — 18 dc counting beg ch.

Rnd 2: Ch 3 for first dc, dc in same st, 2 dc in each st around, sl st to top of beg ch.

Rnd 3: Ch 3 for first dc, * (2 dc in next st, dc in next st) twice, ch 1, sk 1 st **, dc in next st, rep from * 5 times more, end last rep at **, sl st to top of beg ch.

Rnd 4: Ch 3 for first dc, * 2 dc in next st, dc in next st, 5 dc in next st, draw up a lp in last st and drop lp from hook, insert hook in top of first dc of group, pick up dropped lp, draw through and tighten, (popcorn st completed), ch 1, dc in next st, 2 dc in next st, dc in next st, ch 2, sk ch-1 sp **, dc in next st, rep from * around, end last rep at **, sl st to top of beg ch.

Rnd 5: Ch 3 for first dc, * 2 dc in next st, dc in each of next 5 sts, 2 dc in next st, dc in next st, ch 2, sk ch-2 sp **, dc in next st, rep from * around, end last rep at **, sl st to top of beg ch.

Rnd 6: Ch 3 for first dc, * 2 dc in next st, dc in next st, popcorn in next st, dc in each of next 3 sts, popcorn in next st, dc in next st, 2 dc in next st, dc in next st, ch 3, sk next ch-2 sp **, dc in next st, rep from * around, end last rep at **, sl st to top of beg ch.

Rnd 7: Ch 3 for first dc, * (2 dc in next st, dc in each of next 4 sts) twice, 2 dc in next st, dc in next st, ch 4, sk ch-3 sp **, dc in next st, rep from * around, end last rep at **, sl st to top of beg ch. Fasten off.

Assembly: Whipstitch motifs tog, matching popcorn sections, to make a round for pillow top (see photograph).

Finishing: Cut 17″-diameter circles from fabric for front and back. With right sides of fabric circles facing and using ½″ seam, stitch halfway around. Clip curves and turn. Insert pillow form. Turn under seam allowance and slipstitch remainder of circle closed. Place crocheted piece right side up on pillow and tack the outside edges to the pillow with matching thread. Slipstitch beaded trim around edge of pillow at seam.

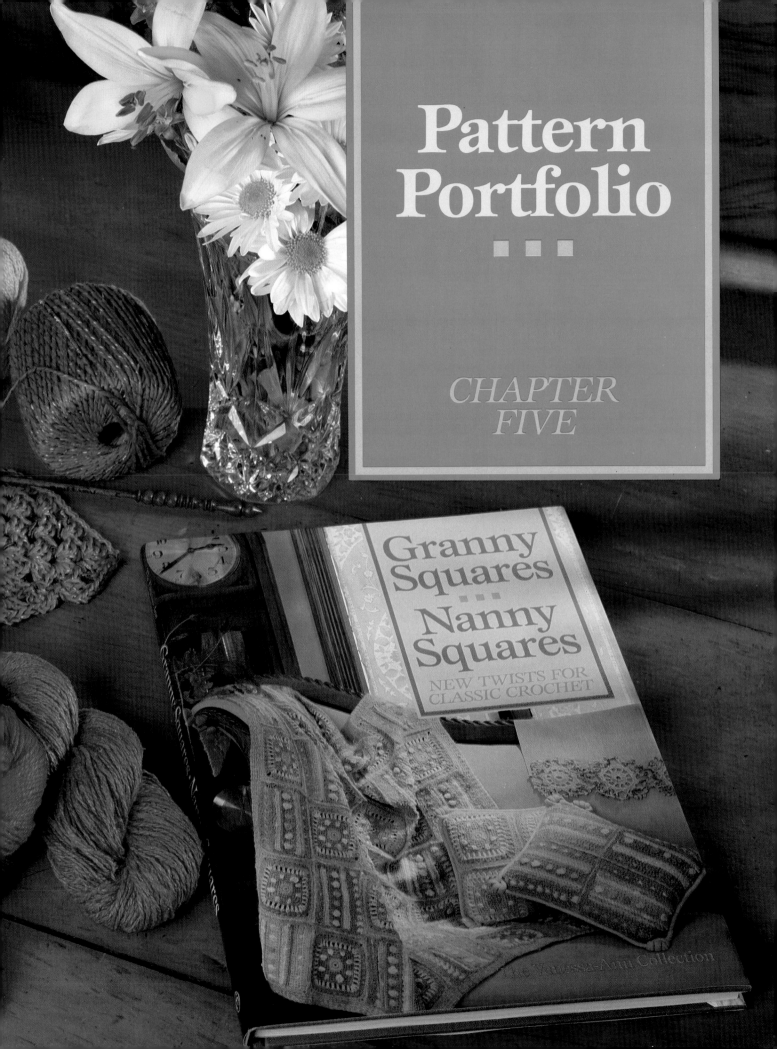

Pattern Portfolio

...

CHAPTER FIVE

ANTIQUE LACE

ANTIQUE LACE

MATERIALS
Size 8 pearl cotton thread: ecru.
Size #12 steel crochet hook, or size to obtain gauge.

GAUGE
Motif = 10″ diameter.

DIRECTIONS
Ch 8, join with a sl st to form a ring.

Rnd 1: Ch 2 for first hdc, 15 hdc in ring, sl st to top of beg ch.

Rnd 2: Ch 3 for first hdc and ch 1, * hdc in next st, ch 1, rep from * around, sl st to 2nd ch of beg ch.

Rnd 3: Ch 3 for first dc, dc in same st, ch 1, * 2 dc in next hdc, ch 1, rep from * around, sl st to top of beg ch.

Rnd 4: Ch 3 for first dc, dc in same st, dc in next dc, ch 1, * 2 dc in next dc, dc in next dc, ch 1, rep from * around, sl st to top of beg ch.

Rnd 5: Ch 3 for first dc, dc in same st, * dc in each of next 2 dc, ch 1 **, 2 dc in next dc, rep from * around, end last rep at **, sl st to top of beg ch.

Rnd 6: Ch 3 for first dc, dc in same st, * dc in each of next 3 dc, ch 1 **, 2 dc in next dc, rep from * around, end last rep at **, sl st to top of beg ch.

Rnd 7: Ch 3 for first dc, dc in each of next 4 dc, * dc in next sp, dc in each of next 5 dc, rep from * around, dc in last sp, sl st to top of beg ch.

Rnd 8: Ch 3 for first dc, dc in each dc around, sl st to top of beg ch.

Rnd 9: Ch 6 for first dc and ch 3, * sk 1 dc, dc in next dc, ch 3, rep from * around, sl st to 3rd ch of beg ch.

Rnd 10: Sl st in next sp, ch 3 for first dc, 3 dc in same sp, * (ch 3, dc in next sp) 5 times, ch 3 **, 4 dc in next sp, rep from * around, end last rep at **, sl st to top of beg ch.

Rnd 11: Sl st in next sp, ch 3 for first dc, 3 dc in same sp, ch 3, * work (dc in next sp, ch 3) 4 times **, (4 dc in next sp, ch 3) twice, rep from * around, end last rep at **, 4 dc in last sp, ch 3, sl st to top of beg ch.

Rnd 12: Sl st in next sp, ch 3 for first dc, 3 dc in same sp, * (ch 3, dc in next sp) 3 times, ch 3, 4 dc in next sp, ch 5, tr in next sp, ch 5 **, 4 dc in next sp, rep from * around, end last rep at **, sl st to top of beg ch.

Rnd 13: Sl st in next sp, ch 3 for first dc, 3 dc in same sp, * ch 3, dc in next dc, ch 3, sk next ch-3 sp, 4 dc in next sp, ch 6, sc in 5th ch of ch-5 sp, sc in tr, sc in first ch of next ch-5 sp, ch 6 **, 4 dc in next ch-3 sp, rep from * around, end last rep at **, sl st to top of beg ch.

Rnd 14: Sl st in next sp, ch 3 for first dc, 3 dc in same sp, * ch 3, 4 dc in next sp, ch 9, sc in 6th ch of ch-6 sp, sc in each of next 3 sc, sc in first ch of next ch-6 sp, ch 9 **, 4 dc in next ch-3 sp, rep from * around, end last rep at **, sl st to top of beg ch.

Rnd 15: Sl st in next sp, ch 3 for first dc, 3 dc in same sp, * ch 3, 4 dc in ch-9 sp, ch 6, sk 1 sc, sc in each of next 3 sc, ch 6, 4 dc in next ch-9 sp, ch 3 **, 4 dc in next ch-3 sp, rep from * around, end last rep at **, sl st to top of beg ch.

Rnd 16: Sl st in next sp, ch 3 for first dc, 3 dc in same sp, * ch 3, 4 dc in ch-6 sp, ch 5, tr in center st of 3-sc group, ch 5, 4 dc in next ch-6 sp, ch 3, 4 dc in next sp, ch 5 **, 4 dc in next sp, rep from * around, end last rep at **, sl st to top of beg ch.

Rnd 17: Sl st in next sp, ch 3 for first dc, 3 dc in same sp, * ch 3, 4 dc in next ch-5 sp, ch 7, sk 4-dc group, ch-3 sp, and 4-dc group, (4 tr, ch 5, 4 tr) in next ch-3 sp (shell completed), ch 7 **, sk next 4-dc group, ch-3 sp, and 4-dc group, 4 dc in next ch-5 sp, rep from * around, end last rep at **, sl st to top of beg ch.

Rnd 18: Sl st in next sp, ch 3 for first dc, 4 dc in same sp, * ch 6, sk 4-dc group, ch-7 sp, and 1 tr, tr in each of next 2 tr, ch 2, shell in next ch-5 sp, ch 2, sk 1 tr, tr in each of next 2 tr, ch 6 **, sk 1 tr, ch-7 sp, and 4-dc group, 5 dc in next ch-3 sp, rep from * around, end last rep at **, sl st to top of beg ch.

Rnd 19: Sl st in next 2 sts, ch 9 for first dc and ch 6, * work (2 tr bet next 2 tr, ch 2) 3 times, shell in next ch-5 sp, ch 2, (2 tr bet next 2 tr, ch 2) twice, 2 tr bet next 2 tr, ch 6 **, dc in center st of next 5-dc group, ch 6, rep from * around, end last rep at **, sl st to 3rd ch of beg ch.

Rnd 20: Ch 9 for first dc and ch 6, * (sk 2-tr group, 2 tr in next ch-2 sp, ch 2) 3 times, sk 2 tr, 2 tr bet next 2 tr, ch 2, shell in next ch-5 sp, ch 2, sk 2 tr, 2 tr bet next 2 tr, ch 2, (sk 2-tr group, 2 tr in next ch-2 sp, ch 2) twice, 2 tr in next ch-2 sp, ch 6 **, dc in next dc, ch 6, rep from * around, end last rep at **, sl st to 3rd ch of beg ch.

Rnd 21: Ch 9 for first dc and ch 6, * (sk 2-tr group, 2 tr in next ch-2 sp, ch 2) 4 times, sk 2 tr, 2 tr bet next 2 tr, ch 2, (4 tr, ch 3, 4 tr) in next ch-5 sp, ch 2, sk 2 tr, 2 tr bet next 2 tr, ch 2, (sk 2-tr group, 2 tr in next ch-2 sp, ch 2) 3 times, 2 tr in next ch-2 sp, ch 6 **, dc in next dc, ch 6, rep from * around, end last rep at **, sl st to 3rd ch of beg ch. Fasten off.

EIGHT SPOKES

FRAMED SQUARE

EIGHT SPOKES

MATERIALS

Size 10 crochet thread: ivory.

Size #8 steel crochet hook, or size to obtain gauge.

GAUGE

Motif = 10″ diameter.

DIRECTIONS

Ch 6, join with a sl st to form a ring.

Rnd 1: Ch 7 for first tr and ch 3, (tr in ring, ch 3) 7 times, sl st to 4th ch of beg ch—8 spokes counting beg ch.

Rnd 2: Sl st in next sp, ch 4 for first tr, 3 tr in same sp, ch 2, * 4 tr in next sp, ch 2, rep from * around, sl st to top of beg ch.

Rnd 3: Ch 4 for first tr, * (tr bet next 2 tr) 3 times, (tr, ch 3, tr) in next sp, rep from * around, sl st to top of beg ch—5 tr in each group.

Rnd 4: Ch 4 for first tr, * (tr bet next 2 tr) 4 times, (tr, ch 5, tr) in next sp, rep from * around, sl st to top of beg ch.

Rnd 5: Sl st in next st, ch 4 for first tr, keeping last lp of each st on hook, work 1 tr bet each of next 4 tr, yo and through all lps on hook (beg cluster completed), * ch 7, tr in center st of next ch-5 sp, ch 7, keeping last lp of each st on hook, work 1 tr bet each of next 5 tr, yo and through all lps on hook (cluster completed), rep from * around, sl st to top of beg ch.

Rnd 6: Ch 4 for first tr, tr in same st, * ch 5, 2 tr in next sp, tr in next tr, 2 tr in next sp, ch 5, 2 tr in top of next cluster, rep from * around, sl st to top of beg ch.

Rnd 7: Ch 4 for first tr, (2 tr, ch 2, 3 tr) bet beg ch and first tr of prev rnd, * ch 5, (tr bet next 2 tr) 4 times, ch 5, (3 tr, ch 2, 3 tr) bet next 2 tr, rep from * around, sl st to top of beg ch.

Rnd 8: Sl st in sp just made, ch 4 for first tr, * tr in each of next 3 tr, (2 tr, ch 2, 2 tr) in next ch-2 sp, tr in each of next 3 tr, tr in next sp, ch 4, (tr bet next 2 sts) 3 times, ch 4, tr in next sp, rep from * around, sl st to top of beg ch.

Rnd 9: Sl st in sp just made, ch 4 for first tr, * tr in each of next 6 tr, (2 tr, ch 1, 2 tr) in next ch-2 sp, tr in each of next 6 sts, tr in next sp, ch 3, (tr bet next 2 sts) twice, ch 3, tr in next sp, rep from * around, sl st to top of beg ch.

Rnd 10: Ch 5 for first dc and ch 2, * (sk 2 tr, dc in next tr, ch 2) twice, sk 1 tr, dc in tr before sp, ch 3, sk next sp, dc in next st, (ch 2, sk 2 tr, dc in next tr) 3 times, 2 dc in next sp, sk 2 tr, 2 dc in next sp, dc in next tr, ch 2, rep from * around, sl st to 3rd ch of beg ch.

Rnd 11: Ch 6 for first dc and ch 3, * (dc in next dc, ch 3) 6 times, (dc bet next 2 sts) twice, sk sp bet next 2 sts, (dc bet next 2 sts) twice, ch 3, rep from * around, sl st to 3rd ch of beg ch.

Rnd 12: Ch 1, sc in same st, * ch 5, (sc in next dc, ch 5) 6 times, (sc bet next 2 dc) 3 times, rep from * around, sl st to first sc. Fasten off.

FRAMED SQUARE

MATERIALS

Size 10 crochet thread: cream.

Size #8 steel crochet hook, or size to obtain gauge.

GAUGE

Motif = 7½″ diameter.

DIRECTIONS

Ch 10, join with a sl st to form a ring.

Rnd 1: Ch 4 for first tr, 23 tr in ring, sl st to top of beg ch.

Rnd 2: Ch 12 for first tr and ch 8, sk 2 tr, tr in next tr, * ch 8, sk 2 tr, tr in next tr, rep from * around, sl st to 4th ch of beg ch—8 lps.

Rnd 3: Sl st in next lp, ch 4 for first tr, 4 tr in same lp, ch 5, sl st in 5th ch from hook to make a picot, 4 tr in same lp, * (5 tr, picot, 4 tr) in next lp, rep from * around, sl st to top of beg ch.

Rnd 4: Ch 18 for first tr and ch 14, sk 8 tr, * tr bet tr groups, ch 14, sk 9 tr, rep from * around, sl st to 4th ch of beg ch.

Rnd 5: Sl st in next lp, ch 3 for first dc, (6 dc, picot, 7 dc) in same lp, * (7 dc, picot, 7 dc) in next lp, rep from * around, sl st to top of beg ch.

Rnd 6: Ch 1, * sc in each of next 7 dc, ch 8, sk picot, sc in each of next 7 dc, ch 16, sk 14 dc, rep from * around, sl st to first sc.

Rnd 7: Sl st in next 2 sc, ch 1, * sc in each of next 5 sc, 8 sc in next lp, sc in each of next 5 sc, ch 7, (6 dc, ch 6, 6 dc) in next lp, ch 7, sk next 2 sc, rep from * around, sl st to first sc.

Rnd 8: Ch 1, * sc in each of next 18 sc, 6 sc in next lp, dc in each of next 6 dc, (3 dc, ch 2, 3 dc) in next ch-6 lp, dc in each of next 6 dc, 6 sc in next lp, rep from * around, sl st to first sc. Fasten off.

PINEAPPLE DOILY

MATERIALS

Size 20 crochet thread: ivory.

Size #10 steel crochet hook, or size to obtain gauge.

GAUGE

Motif = 8½″ diameter.

DIRECTIONS

Rnd 1: * Ch 6, sl st in 5th ch from hook to make a picot, rep from * 7 times more, join with a sl st to form a ring. Turn picots to inside of ring.

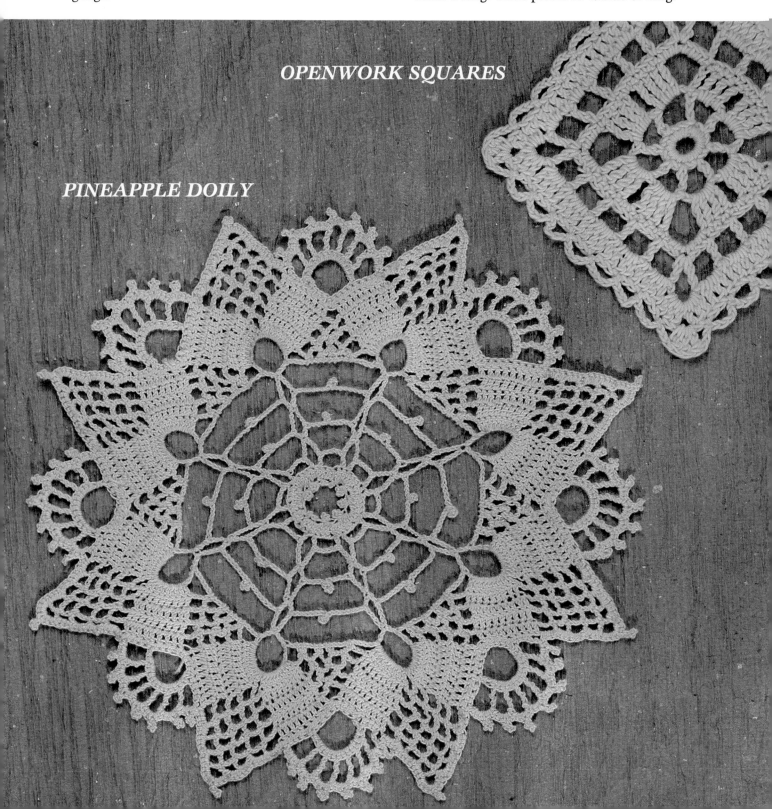

OPENWORK SQUARES

PINEAPPLE DOILY

Rnd 2: Sl st to base of next picot, ch 3 for first dc, dc in same picot, 3 dc in next ch-1 sp, (2 dc in base of next picot, 3 dc in next ch-1 sp) 7 times, sl st to top of beg ch—40 dc counting beg ch.

Rnd 3: Ch 10 for first dc and ch 7, dc in next st, (ch 4, sk 3 dc, dc in next dc, ch 7, dc in next dc) 7 times, ch 4, sl st to 3rd ch of beg ch.

Rnd 4: Sl st to center of next ch-7 lp, ch 11 for first dc and ch 8, * sl st in 5th ch from hook to make a picot, ch 4, sk next ch-4 sp, (dc, ch 7, dc) in 4th ch of next ch-7 lp, ch 8, rep from * 6 times more, sl st in 5th ch from hook to make a picot, ch 4, dc in first sl st, ch 4, tr in 3rd ch of beg ch.

Rnd 5: Ch 15 for first dc and ch 12, * sl st in 5th ch from hook to make a picot, ch 7, sk picot lp, (dc, ch 9, dc) in 4th ch of next ch-7 lp, ch 12, rep from * 6 times more, sl st in 5th ch from hook to make a picot, ch 7, dc in tr, ch 5, tr in 3rd ch of beg ch.

Rnd 6: Ch 23 for first dc and ch 20, dc in same st, * ch 16, sk picot lp, (dc, ch 20, dc) in 5th ch of next ch-9 lp, rep from * 6 times more, ch 16, sl st to 3rd ch of beg ch.

Rnd 7: Sl st in next lp, ch 3 for first dc, (8 dc, ch 5, 9 dc) in same lp, * ch 3, sc in next lp, (ch 5, sc in same lp) 3 times, ch 3 **, (9 dc, ch 5, 9 dc) in next lp, rep from * around, end last rep at **, sl st to top of beg ch.

Rnd 8: Ch 3 for first dc, dc in each of next 8 dc, * ch 5, sc in next ch-5 lp, ch 5, dc in each of next 9 dc, ch 3, sc in next ch-5 lp, (ch 5, sc in next ch-5 lp) twice, ch 3 **, dc in each of next 9 dc, rep from * around, end last rep at **, sl st to top of beg ch.

Rnd 9: Ch 3 for first dc, dc in each of next 8 dc, * (ch 5, sc in next lp) twice, ch 5, dc in each of next 9 dc, ch 3, sc in next ch-5 lp, ch 5, sc in next ch-5 lp, ch 3 **, dc in each of next 9 dc, rep from * around, end last rep at **, sl st to top of beg ch.

Rnd 10: Ch 3 for first dc, dc in each of next 8 dc, * (ch 5, sc in next lp) 3 times, ch 5, dc in each of next 9 dc, ch 3, sc in next ch-5 lp, ch 3 **, dc in each of next 9 dc, rep from * around, end last rep at **, sl st to top of beg ch.

Rnd 11: Ch 3 for first dc, dc in each of next 8 dc, * (ch 5, sc in next lp) 4 times, turn, ch 5, sc in lp, (ch 5, sc in next lp) twice, ch 2, dc in next lp, turn, (ch 5, sc in next lp) twice, ch 2, dc in next lp, turn, ch 5, sc in next lp, ch 2, dc in next lp, turn, ch 5, sc in next lp, sl st to lp before next dc, ch 3, dc in each of next 9 dc **, sk sc, dc in each of next 9 dc, rep from * around, end last rep at **, sl st to top of beg ch. Fasten off.

Rnd 12: Join thread in st 9 dc before last sl st, ch 1, sc in each of next 13 sts, * ch 12, turn, sk 8 sc, sc in next sc, turn, 13 sc in ch-12 lp just made, sc in each of next 4 dc of prev rnd, turn, sk 4 sc just made, (ch 3, sk 1 sc, tr in next sc) 6 times, ch 3, sk 3 sc, sc in next sc, turn, (2 sc, ch 5, sl st in 5th ch from hook to make a picot, 2 sc) in lp just made, (2 sc, picot, 2 sc) in each of next 6 lps, 3 sc in each of next 4 lps, (3 sc, picot, 3 sc) in lp at point, 3 sc in each of next 4 lps **, sc in each of next 14 sts, rep from * around, end last rep at **, sl st to first sc. Fasten off.

OPENWORK SQUARES

MATERIALS
Size 10 crochet thread: ecru.
Size #6 steel crochet hook, or size to obtain gauge.

GAUGE
Square = 4″.

DIRECTIONS
Ch 8, join with a sl st to form a ring.

Rnd 1: Ch 1, 16 sc in ring, sl st to first sc.

Rnd 2: Ch 7 for first tr and ch 3, (sk 1 st, tr in next st, ch 3) 7 times, sl st to 4th ch of beg ch.

Rnd 3: Ch 4 for first tr, 3 tr in same sp, ch 1, 4 tr in next sp, ch 5 for corner, * 4 tr in next sp, ch 1, 4 tr in next sp, ch 5 for corner, rep from * around, sl st to top of beg ch.

Rnd 4: Ch 1, * sc evenly to next corner, 6 sc in corner, rep from * around, sl st to first sc.

Rnd 5: Ch 6 for first dc and ch 3, (sk 2 sc, dc in next sc, ch 3) 3 times, * sk 2 sc, (dc, ch 4, dc) in next sc for corner **, (ch 3, sk 2 sc, dc in next sc) 4 times, ch 3, rep from * around, end last rep at **, ch 3, sl st to 3rd ch of beg ch.

Rnd 6: Ch 3 for first dc, (3 dc in next sp, dc in next dc) 4 times, * work (3 dc, ch 3, 3 dc) in corner, (3 dc in next sp, dc in next dc) 4 times, rep from * around, sl st to top of beg ch.

Rnd 7: * (Ch 5, sk 2 dc, sc in next dc) to next corner, ch 3, 3 dc in corner, ch 3, sk 1 dc, sc in next dc, rep from * around, ch 5, sl st to base of beg ch. Fasten off.

FOUR HEARTS

KALEIDOSCOPE

FOUR HEARTS

MATERIALS
Worsted-weight brushed acrylic: white.
Worsted-weight acrylic-mohair blend: pink.
Size F crochet hook, or size to obtain gauge.

GAUGE
Square = 6½".

DIRECTIONS
Note: Carry color not in use across row by working over it with the next group of sts. To avoid holes when changing colors, bring up new color from under dropped color. Always bring up new color as last yo of old color.

Square: With white, ch 6, join with a sl st to form a ring.

Rnd 1: Ch 4 for first dc and ch 1, * 4 dc in ring, drop lp from hook, insert hook in first dc of group, pick up dropped lp, draw through and tighten (popcorn st completed), ch 1, dc in ring, ch 1, rep from * twice more, end with popcorn, ch 1, sl st to 3rd ch of beg ch.

Rnd 2: Ch 3 for first dc, dc in next ch-1 sp, ch 2, * keeping last lp of each st on hook, work 3 dc in top of popcorn, yo and through all lps on hook (cluster completed), ch 2, cluster in same popcorn, ch 2, dc in next sp, dc in next dc, dc in next sp, ch 2, rep from * around, sl st to top of beg ch. Drop white, but do not fasten off.

Rnd 3: Join pink and ch 3 for first dc, with white, dc in next st, dc in next sp, ch 2, * (cluster, ch 2, cluster) in corner ch-2 sp, ch 2, dc in next sp, dc in next dc, with pink, dc in next dc, with white, dc in next dc, dc in next sp, ch 2, rep from * around, with pink, sl st to top of beg ch.

Rnd 4: With pink, ch 3 for first dc, dc in next dc, with white, dc in next dc, dc in next sp, * ch 2, (cluster, ch 2, cluster) in corner ch-2 sp, ch 2, dc in next sp, dc in next dc, with pink, dc in each of next 3 dc, with white, dc in next dc, dc in next sp, rep from * around, with pink, dc in last dc, sl st to top of beg ch.

Rnd 5: With pink, ch 3 for first dc, dc in each of next 2 dc, with white, dc in next dc, dc in next sp, ch 2, * (cluster, ch 2, cluster) in corner, ch 2, dc in next sp, dc in next dc, with pink, dc in each of next 5 dc, with white, dc in next dc, dc in next sp, ch 2, rep from * around, with pink, dc in last 2 dc, sl st to top of beg ch.

Rnd 6: With white, ch 3 for first dc, with pink, dc in each of next 3 dc, with white, dc in next dc, dc in next sp, ch 2, * (cluster, ch 2, cluster) in corner, ch 2, dc in next sp, dc in next dc, with pink, dc in each of next 3 dc, with white, dc in next sp, with pink, dc in each of next 3 dc, with white, dc in next dc, dc in next sp, ch 2, rep from * around, sl st to top of beg ch. Fasten off pink.

Rnd 7: With white, ch 3 for first dc, * dc in each dc to next corner, ch 2, (cluster, ch 2, cluster) in corner, ch 2, rep from * around, sl st to top of beg ch. Fasten off.

Finishing: With right side facing, join 1 strand of pink at point of heart and work 12 surface ch sts around edge of each heart.

KALEIDOSCOPE

MATERIALS
Fingering-weight acrylic: blue, green, pink, purple.
Size G crochet hook, or size to obtain gauge.

GAUGE
Square = 3½".

DIRECTIONS
With blue, ch 6, join with a sl st to form a ring.

Rnd 1: Ch 3 for first dc, 2 dc in ring, (ch 2 for corner, 3 dc in ring) 3 times, ch 2 for last corner, sl st to top of beg ch. Fasten off.

Rnd 2: Join green in any corner ch-2 sp, ch 3 for first dc, (dc, ch 2, 2 dc) in same corner, * dc in next dc, yo and insert hook in center of ring, draw up a long lp, complete st as a dc (long dc completed), dc in next dc, (2 dc, ch 2, 2 dc) in next corner, rep from * around, sl st to top of beg ch. Fasten off.

Rnd 3: Join pink in any corner, ch 3 for first dc, (dc, ch 2, 2 dc) in same corner, * dc in each of next 2 dc, long dc in top of next dc of rnd 1, dc in next dc, long dc in top of next dc of rnd 1, dc in each of next 2 dc, (2 dc, ch 2, 2 dc) in corner, rep from * around, sl st to top of beg ch. Fasten off.

Rnd 4: Join purple in any corner, * (2 sc, ch 2, 2 sc) in same corner, sc evenly to next corner, rep from * around, sl st to first sc. Fasten off.

WINDMILL

MATERIALS
Worsted-weight cotton: ivory.
Size F crochet hook, or size to obtain gauge.

GAUGE
Square = 5″.

DIRECTIONS
Ch 8, join with a sl st to form a ring.

Rnd 1: Ch 4 for first tr, 3 tr in ring, ch 6 for corner, (4 tr in ring, ch 6 for corner) 3 times, sl st to top of beg ch.

Rnd 2: Ch 4 for first tr, * tr in each tr to next corner, (3 tr, ch 3, 3 tr) in corner, rep from * around, sl st to top of beg ch.

WINDMILL

PINK PEONY

RUFFLES

Rnd 3: Ch 5 for first tr and ch 1, (sk 1 tr, tr in next tr, ch 1) 3 times, * (tr, ch 2, tr, ch 2, tr) in corner, (ch 1, sk 1 tr, tr in next tr) 5 times, ch 1, rep from * around, sl st to 4th ch of beg ch. Fasten off.

PINK PEONY

MATERIALS
Fingering-weight acrylic: off-white.
Sportweight brushed acrylic: pink.
Size F crochet hook, or size to obtain gauge.

GAUGE
Square = 6″.

DIRECTIONS
Square: With off-white, ch 8, join with a sl st to form a ring.

Rnd 1: Ch 4 for first tr, 15 tr in ring, sl st to top of beg ch—16 tr counting beg ch.

Rnd 2: Ch 1, * (sc, hdc, dc, tr, dc, hdc, sc) in next tr, sk 1 tr, rep from * around, sl st to first sc.

Rnd 3: Ch 1, * holding petal to front of work, insert hook through 2 lps on back of next tr on rnd 1, (sc, hdc, dc, 2 tr, dc, hdc, sc) in same st, rep from * around, sl st to first sc.

Rnd 4: Sl st to center st of next petal, sl st bet 2 tr, ch 3 for first dc, (2 dc, ch 2, 3 dc) in same sp, * ch 2, (3 dc, ch 2) 3 times bet 2 tr of next petal for corner **, (3 dc, ch 2, 3 dc) bet 2 tr of next petal, rep from * around, end last rep at **, sl st to top of beg ch.

Rnd 5: Sl st in next sp, ch 3 for first dc, 2 dc in same sp, * 3 dc in each sp to next corner, (3 dc, ch 3, 3 dc) in center st of corner 3-dc group, rep from * around, sl st to top of beg ch.

Rnd 6: Ch 3 for first dc, * dc evenly to next corner, (3 dc, ch 3, 3 dc) in corner, rep from * around, sl st to top of beg ch. Fasten off.

Pink flower: With pink, ch 6, join with a sl st to form a ring.

Rnd 1: * (Draw up a ¾″ lp, ch 1, sc bet single back strand and 2 front strands of lp) twice (lp st completed), sl st in bk lp of next ch on ring, rep from * 5 times more, sc in first lp of ring.

Rnd 2: Work (lp st, sc in next ft lp of ring) 6 times, sl st to first sc.

Fasten off leaving a tail of yarn. Use tail to sew flower to center of square.

RUFFLES

MATERIALS
Fingering-weight acrylic: pale yellow.
Worsted-weight acrylic-nylon blend: white.
Sizes E and G crochet hooks, or size to obtain gauge.

GAUGE
Square = 5½″.

DIRECTIONS
Square: With size E hook and pale yellow, ch 6, join with a sl st to form a ring.

Rnd 1: Ch 4 for first dc and ch 1, * keeping last lp of each st on hook, work 3 dc in ring, yo and through all lps on hook (cluster completed), ch 2, cluster in ring, ch 1, dc in ring, ch 1, rep from * twice more, cluster, ch 2, cluster, ch 1, sl st to 3rd ch of beg ch.

Rnd 2: Ch 3 for first dc, dc in next ch-1 sp, ch 1, * (cluster, ch 2, cluster) in next ch-2 sp for corner, ch 1, dc in next ch-1 sp **, dc in next dc, dc in next ch-1 sp, ch 1, rep from * around, end last rep at **, sl st to top of beg ch.

Rnd 3: Ch 3 for first dc, dc in next dc, dc in next ch-1 sp, ch 1, * (cluster, ch 2, cluster) in corner, ch 1, dc in next ch-1 sp **, dc in each of next 3 dc, dc in next ch-1 sp, ch 1, rep from * around, end last rep at **, dc in last dc, sl st to top of beg ch.

Rnd 4: Ch 3 for first dc, dc in each of next 2 dc, dc in next ch-1 sp, ch 1, * (cluster, ch 2, cluster) in corner, ch 1, dc in next ch-1 sp **, dc in each of next 5 dc, dc in next ch-1 sp, ch 1, rep from * around, end last rep at **, dc in each of last 2 dc, sl st to top of beg ch.

Rnds 5 and 6: Ch 3 for first dc, * dc evenly to next corner, ch 1, (cluster, ch 2, cluster) in corner, ch 1, rep from * around, sl st to top of beg ch. Fasten off after rnd 6.

Ruffle: With size G hook and right side of square facing, join white around post of any dc on rnd 3, sc around same post, ch 3, sc around same post, * sc around next post, ch 3, sc around same post, rep from * around each dc and cluster post of rnd 3, join with sl st to first sc. Fasten off.

Rep ruffle on rnd 5.

PASSION FLOWER

MATERIALS

Worsted-weight acrylic: teal, plum, blue, green, black.

Size I crochet hook, or size to obtain gauge.

GAUGE

Motif = 6½″ diameter.

DIRECTIONS

With teal, ch 6, join with a sl st to form a ring.

Rnd 1: Ch 2 for first hdc, 11 hdc in ring, sl st to top of beg ch. Fasten off.

PASSION FLOWER

CLUSTERS & ARCHES

SWEETHEART ROSE

Rnd 2: Join plum in any hdc. Draw up ½" lp, yo, draw up lp, yo and through all lps on hook (beg puff st completed), ch 1, (yo and draw up a lp) twice in next st, yo and through all lps on hook (puff st completed), * ch 3, puff st in next hdc, ch 1, puff st in next hdc, rep from * around, ch 3, sl st to top of first puff st. Fasten off.

Rnd 3: Join blue in any ch-3 sp, ch 3 for first dc, (dc, tr, ch 3, tr, 2 dc) in same ch-3 sp, sc in ch-1 sp, * (2 dc, tr, ch 3, tr, 2 dc) in next ch-3 sp, sc in next ch-1 sp, rep from * around, sl st to top of beg ch. Fasten off.

Rnd 4: Join green in any ch-3 sp, ch 3 for first dc, (2 dc, ch 3, 3 dc) in same sp, * ch 3, tr in next sc, ch 3 **, (3 dc, ch 3, 3 dc) in next ch-3 sp, rep from * around, end last rep at **, sl st to top of beg ch. Fasten off.

Rnd 5: Join black in ch-3 sp bet any 3-dc groups, ch 3 for first dc, (2 dc, ch 2, 3 dc) in same sp, ch 1, * (3 dc in next sp) twice, ch 1, (3 dc, ch 2, 3 dc) in next sp, ch 1, rep from * around, sl st to top of beg ch. Fasten off.

CLUSTERS & ARCHES

MATERIALS
Sportweight wool-acrylic blend slubbed texture: multicolor black, green, and blue.
Size F crochet hook, or size to obtain gauge.

GAUGE
Square = 6".

DIRECTIONS
Ch 8, join with a sl st to form a ring.

Rnd 1: Ch 1, 15 sc in ring, sl st to first sc.

Rnd 2: Ch 3 for first dc, keeping last lp of each st on hook, work 2 dc in same st, yo and through all lps on hook (beg cluster completed), * ch 3, sk 1 st, keeping last lp of each st on hook, work 3 dc in next st, yo and through all lps on hook (cluster completed), rep from * 6 times more, ch 3, sl st to top of first cluster.

Rnd 3: Ch 3 for first dc, work beg cluster in same st, * ch 3, sc in next ch-3 sp, ch 3 **, cluster in top of next cluster, rep from * 6 times more, end last rep at **, sl st to top of first cluster.

Rnd 4: Ch 7 for first dc and ch 4, dc in same st, * ch 3, dc in next sc, ch 5, sk next cluster, dc in next sc, ch 3, (dc, ch 4, dc) in next cluster for corner, rep from * around, sl st to 3rd ch of beg ch.

Rnd 5: Ch 3 for first dc, work beg cluster in same st, ch 3, cluster in same st, ch 1, sk ch-4 sp, (cluster, ch 3, cluster) in next dc, * ch 3, cluster in next dc, ch 3, dc in next ch-5 sp, ch 3, cluster in next dc, ch 3, (cluster, ch 3, cluster) in next dc, ch 1, (cluster, ch 3, cluster) in next dc, rep from * around, sl st to top of first cluster.

Rnd 6: Ch 1, sc in same st, * ch 6, sk 1 cluster, (cluster, ch 3, cluster) in next ch-1 sp, ch 4, sk 1 cluster, (sc in top of next cluster, ch 4) twice, sc in next dc, (ch 4, sc in top of next cluster) twice, rep from * around, sl st to first sc.

Rnd 7: Ch 1, work 5 sc in each ch-4 sp around, sl st to first sc. Fasten off.

SWEETHEART ROSE

MATERIALS
Fingering-weight cotton: dark rust, medium rust.
Size #4 steel crochet hook, or size to obtain gauge.

GAUGE
Motif = 4½" diameter.

DIRECTIONS
With dark rust, ch 8, join with a sl st to form a ring.

Rnd 1: Ch 1, 12 sc in ring, sl st to first sc.

Rnd 2: Ch 3 for first dc, working in bk lps only, 2 dc in same st, (ch 3, sk 1 sc, 3 dc in next sc) 5 times, ch 3, sk 1 sc, sl st to top of beg ch.

Rnd 3: Sl st in next st, ch 1, sc in same st, * sk next st, 9 dc in next ch-3 sp **, sk 1 st, sc in next st, rep from * around, end last rep at **, sl st to first sc. Fasten off.

Rnd 4: Join medium rust in center st of any 9-dc group, ch 8 for first dc and ch 5, dc in same st, * ch 8, (dc, ch 5, dc) in center dc of next 9-dc group, rep from * around, ch 8, sl st to 3rd ch of beg ch.

Rnd 5: Ch 1, * 5 sc in next sp, 9 sc in next sp, rep from * around, sl st to first sc. Fasten off.

Rnd 6: Join dark rust in center st of any 5-sc group, ch 7 for first dc and ch 4, dc in same st, * ch 3, sk 3 sts, dc in next st, (ch 3, sk 2 sts, dc in next st) twice, ch 3, sk 3 sts **, (dc, ch 4, dc) in next st, rep from * around, end last rep at **, sl st to 3rd ch of beg ch.

Rnd 7: Ch 1, * (2 sc, ch 1, 2 sc) in next ch-4 sp, 4 sc in each of next 4 sps, rep from * around, sl st to first sc. Fasten off.

GRANNY LACE

MATERIALS
Sportweight wool: peacock, teal.
Size #0 steel crochet hook, or size to obtain gauge.

GAUGE
Square = 5".

DIRECTIONS
Square: With peacock, ch 6, join with a sl st to form a ring.

Rnd 1: Ch 3 for first dc, 2 dc in ring, (ch 2, 3 dc in ring) 3 times, ch 2, sl st to top of beg ch.

Rnd 2: Ch 3 for first dc, dc in each of next 2 dc, * (dc, ch 2, dc) in ch-2 sp for corner, dc in each of next 3 dc, rep from * twice more, (dc, ch 2, dc) in last corner, sl st to top of beg ch.

Rnd 3: Ch 3 for first dc, * dc in each dc to next corner, (2 dc, ch 2, 2 dc) in corner, rep from * around, sl st to top of beg ch.

Rnds 4-6: Rep rnd 3. Fasten off after rnd 6.

Lace: With teal, ch 4, join with a sl st to form a ring.

Rnd 1: Ch 6 for first tr and ch 2, tr in ring, * ch 4, (tr, ch 2, tr) in ring, rep from * twice more, ch 4, sl st to 4th ch of beg ch.

Rnd 2: Sl st in next ch-2 sp, ch 3 for first dc, (dc, ch 4, 2 dc) in same sp for corner, * ch 2, dc in next ch-4 sp, ch 2, (2 dc, ch 4, 2 dc) in next corner, rep from * twice more, ch 2, dc in ch-4 sp, ch 2, sl st to top of beg ch.

Rnd 3: Sl st in next dc and ch-4 sp, ch 4, for first tr, (tr, ch 4, 2 tr) in same corner sp, * ch 1, sk 1 dc, tr in next dc, (ch 2, tr in next dc) twice, ch 1, sk 1 dc, (2 tr, ch 4, 2 tr) in corner, rep from * around, sl st to top of beg ch.

Rnd 4: Ch 5 for first tr and ch 1, * sk 1 tr, (2 tr, ch 4, 2 tr) in corner, ch 1, sk 1 tr, tr in next tr, ch 1, tr in next tr, (ch 2, tr in next tr) twice, ch 1, tr in next tr, ch 1, rep from * around, sl st to top of beg ch. Fasten off.

Finishing: Sew lace piece to right side of square, joining edges of lace to base of rnd 6 on square. Tack centers of squares tog.

LAVENDER

MATERIALS
Bulky-weight cotton-mohair blend novelty texture: multicolor purple, aqua, and off-white (A).
Bulky-weight mohair blend: off-white (B).
Worsted-weight acrylic-mohair blend: aqua (C).
Size G crochet hook, or size to obtain gauge.

GAUGE
Square = 9".

DIRECTIONS
With A, ch 4, join with a sl st to form a ring.

Rnd 1: Ch 3 for first dc, dc in ring, * ch 6, keeping last lp of each st on hook, work 2 dc in ring, yo and through all lps on hook (2-dc cluster completed), rep from * twice more, ch 6, sl st to top of beg ch.

Rnd 2: Sl st in next sp, ch 4 for first dc and ch 1, (dc in same sp, ch 1) 3 times, dc in same sp, * ch 3, (dc in same sp, ch 1) 4 times, dc in same sp, rep from * around, end with ch 3, sl st to 3rd ch of beg ch. Fasten off.

Rnd 3: Join B in dc before ch-3 sp, ch 8 for first dc and ch 5, * dc in next dc, (2 dc in next ch-1 sp) 4 times, dc in next dc, ch 5 for corner, rep from * around, sl st to 3rd ch of beg ch. Fasten off.

Rnd 4: Join C in dc before ch-5 corner, ch 10 for first dc and ch 7, * dc in next dc, ch 2, sk 1 dc, dc bet next 2 dc, (ch 2, sk 2 dc, dc bet next 2 dc) 3 times, ch 2, dc in next dc, ch 7 for corner, rep from * around, sl st to 3rd ch of beg ch. Fasten off.

Rnd 5: Join A in any corner, * sc in corner, ch 3, [keeping last lp of each st on hook, work 4 dc in next ch-2 sp, yo and through all lps on hook (4-dc cluster completed), ch 2] 4 times, 4-dc cluster in next ch-2 sp, ch 3, rep from * around, sl st to first sc. Fasten off.

Rnd 6: Join C in ch-3 sp before any corner sc, 2 sc in same ch-3 sp, * ch 7 for corner, 2 sc in next ch-3 sp, (sc in top of cluster, 2 sc in ch-2 sp) 4 times, sc in top of cluster, 2 sc in ch-3 sp, rep from * around, sl st to first sc. Fasten off.

Rnd 7: Join B in any corner, * sc in corner, ch 3, sl st in 3rd ch from hook to make a picot, (3 sc, picot) twice in same corner, sc in same corner, sc in each of next 2 sc, picot, (sc in each of next 3 sc, picot) 4 times, sc in each of next 3 sc, rep from * around, sl st to first sc. Fasten off.

GRANNY LACE

LAVENDER

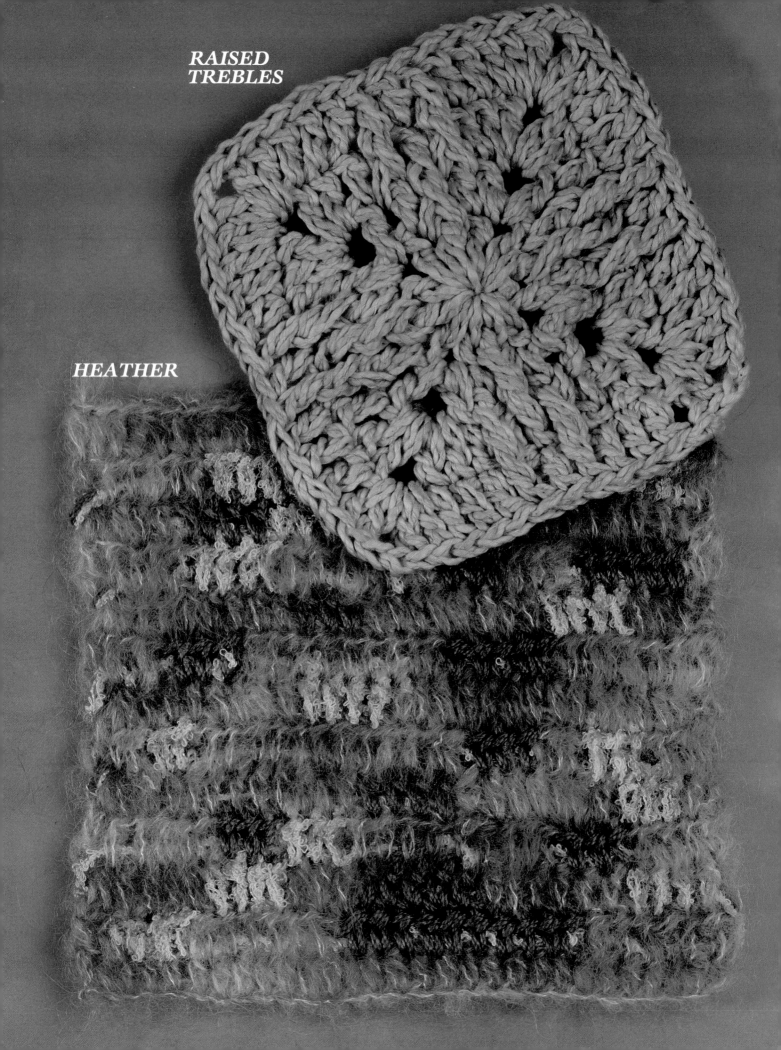

RAISED
TREBLES

HEATHER

HEATHER

MATERIALS
Worsted-weight brushed wool-blend: multicolor purple and aqua (A).
Worsted-weight cotton-blend bouclé: multicolor off-white, pink, and blue (B).
Worsted-weight cotton: purple (C).
Size G crochet hook, or size to obtain gauge.

GAUGE
Square = 8".

DIRECTIONS
Note: Carry color not in use across the row by working over it with the next group of sts. To avoid holes when changing colors, bring up new color from under dropped color. Always bring up new color as last yo of old color.

Square: With A, ch 30.
Row 1: Hdc in 2nd ch from hook and each ch across. Ch 2, turn.
Row 2: Hdc in next st, join B and work 3 hdc, with A, work 7 hdc, join C and work 10 hdc, with A, work 7 hdc. Ch 2, turn.
Row 3: Hdc in next st, with B, work 3 hdc, with A, work 6 hdc, with C, work 5 hdc, with A, work 3 hdc, with B, work 4 hdc, with A, work 6 hdc. Ch 2, turn.
Row 4: Hdc across as follows: 5 A, 3 C, 3 B, 9 A, 3 C, 5 A. Ch 2, turn.
Row 5: Hdc across as follows: 1 A, 3 B, 7 A, 4 C, 13 A. Ch 2, turn.
Row 6: Hdc across as follows: 2 A, 2 B, 12 A, 3 C, 2 A, 3 B, 4 A. Ch 2, turn.
Row 7: Hdc across as follows: 14 A, 4 B, 10 A. Ch 2, turn.
Row 8: Hdc across as follows: 3 A, 3 C, 9 A, 5 C, 8 A. Ch 2, turn.
Row 9: Hdc across as follows: 3 A, 4 B, 8 A, 3 C, 10 A. Ch 2, turn.
Row 10: Hdc across as follows: 4 A, 4 B, 7 A, 3 C, 3 A, 5 C, 2 A. Ch 2, turn.
Row 11: Hdc across as follows: 15 A, 4 B, 4 C, 5 A. Ch 2, turn.
Row 12: Hdc across as follows: 5 A, 4 B, 3 A, 5 C, 6 A, 3 B, 2 A. Ch 2, turn. Fasten off B and C.
Row 13: With A, hdc in each st across the row. Fasten off.

RAISED TREBLES

MATERIALS
Worsted-weight cotton: light gray, light green.
Size G crochet hook, or size to obtain gauge.

GAUGE
Square = 5½".

DIRECTIONS
Note: Work with 1 strand each of light gray and light green held tog as one.

Square: Ch 6, join with a sl st to form a ring.
Rnd 1: Ch 3 for first dc, 2 dc in ring, (ch 2, 3 dc in ring) 3 times, ch 2, sl st to top of beg ch.
Rnd 2: Ch 3 for first dc, dc in each of next 2 dc, * (dc, ch 2, dc) in next ch-2 sp for corner, dc in each of next 3 dc, rep from * twice more, (dc, ch 2, dc) in last corner, sl st to top of beg ch.
Rnd 3: Ch 3 for first dc, yo twice, insert hook from in front and from right to left around post of next dc of rnd 1, complete st as tr (1 tr/raised front completed), dc in each of next 2 dc, * (2 dc, ch 2, 2 dc) in corner, dc in each of next 2 dc, 1 tr/rf around post of next dc of rnd 1, dc in each of next 2 dc, rep from * around, sl st to top of beg ch.
Rnd 4: Sl st in next st, ch 3 for first dc, * 1 tr/rf around post of next dc of rnd 2, dc in each of next 3 dc, (2 dc, ch 2, 2 dc) in corner, dc in each of next 3 dc, 1 tr/rf around post of next dc of rnd 2, dc in next st, rep from * around, sl st to top of beg ch. Fasten off.

BELLS

MATERIALS

Size 10 crochet thread: white.
Size #8 steel crochet hook, or size to obtain gauge.

GAUGE

Square = 3″.

DIRECTIONS

Ch 8, join with a sl st to form a ring.

Rnd 1: Ch 1, 16 sc in ring, sl st to first sc.

Rnd 2: Ch 4 for first tr, 5 tr in same st, * ch 5, sk 3 sc, 6 tr in next st for corner, rep from * twice more, ch 5, sl st to top of beg ch.

Rnd 3: * Sc in each of next 3 tr, ch 5, sl st in 5th ch from hook to make a picot, sc in each of next 3 tr, ch 5, work (tr, ch 4, tr) in next lp, ch 5, rep from * 3 times more, sl st to first sc.

BELLS

POPCORN GRANNY

BUTTERFLY

Rnd 4: Ch 9 for first tr and ch 5, sk 5 sc, tr in next sc, * ch 5, work (3 dc, ch 3, 3 dc) in corner ch-4 lp, ch 5 **, tr in next sc, ch 5, sk 5 sc, tr in next sc, rep from * around, end last rep at **, sl st to 4th ch of beg ch.

Rnd 5: Ch 1, * (4 sc in next sp) twice, sc in each of next 3 dc, 3 sc in corner sp, sc in each of next 3 dc, 4 sc in next sp, rep from * around, sl st to first sc. Fasten off.

BUTTERFLY

MATERIALS
Worsted-weight cotton: white.
Size J crochet hook, or size to obtain gauge.

GAUGE
Square = 7".

DIRECTIONS
Ch 4, join with a sl st to form a ring.

Rnd 1: Ch 1, (sc in ring, ch 5) 4 times, sl st to first sc.

Rnd 2: * Ch 3, (dc, ch 3, dc) in next lp, ch 3, sl st in next sc, rep from * 3 times more, sl st in base of beg ch.

Rnd 3: Work * 3 sc in next ch-3 sp, ch 5, 3 dc in next ch-3 sp, ch 5, 3 sc in next ch-3 sp, rep from * around, sl st to first sc.

Rnd 4: * Ch 5, sc in next lp, ch 3, sk 1 dc, keeping last lp of each st on hook, work 3 dc in center st of 3-dc group, yo and through all lps on hook (cluster completed), ch 3, sc in next lp **, ch 5, sk 3 sc, sl st bet 3-sc groups, rep from * around, end last rep at **, ch 2, dc in base of beg ch.

Rnd 5: Sc in lp just made, * ch 5, sc in next lp, ch 3, sc in next lp, (ch 3, sc in top of cluster) twice **, (ch 3, sc in next lp) twice, rep from * around, end last rep at **, ch 3, sc in next lp, ch 3, sl st to first sc.

Rnd 6: Sl st in next lp, ch 3 for first dc, 3 dc in same lp, * 2 dc in each of next 2 lps, ch 2, (2 dc, ch 1, 2 dc) in corner lp, ch 2, 2 dc in each of next 2 lps **, 4 dc in next ch-5 lp, rep from * around, end last rep at **, sl st to top of beg ch.

Rnd 7: Sc in same st, * ch 3, sk 2 dc, sc in next dc, (ch 3, sk 1 dc, sc in next dc) twice, ch 3, sk ch-2 sp, sc in next dc, ch 3, sk 1 dc, sc in corner ch-1 sp, ch 3, sk 1 dc, sc in next dc, ch 3, sk ch-2 sp, sc in next dc, (ch 3, sk 1 dc, sc in next dc) twice, rep from * around, sl st to first sc. Fasten off.

POPCORN GRANNY

MATERIALS
Sportweight cotton: blue.
Sportweight brushed acrylic: white.
Size #0 steel crochet hook, or size to obtain gauge.

GAUGE
Square = 5".

DIRECTIONS
Popcorn st: Work 4 dc in same st, draw up a lp in last st of group and drop lp from hook, insert hook in first dc of group, pick up dropped lp, draw through and tighten. To beg a rnd with a popcorn, ch 3 for first dc and work 3 dc in same st, complete st as usual.

Square: With blue, ch 4, join with a sl st to form a ring.

Rnd 1: (Popcorn, ch 2 for corner) 4 times, sl st to top of first popcorn. Fasten off.

Rnd 2: Join white in top of any popcorn, ch 3 for first dc, (2 dc, ch 2, 3 dc) in same st for corner, * ch 2, popcorn in next ch-2 sp, ch 2 **, (3 dc, ch 2, 3 dc) in top of next popcorn for corner, rep from * around, end last rep at **, sl st to top of beg ch. Fasten off.

Rnd 3: Join blue in any corner, ch 3 for first dc, (2 dc, ch 2, 3 dc) in same corner, * (ch 2, popcorn in next ch-2 sp) twice, ch 2 **, (3 dc, ch 2, 3 dc) in corner, rep from * around, end last rep at **, sl st to top of beg ch. Fasten off.

Rnd 4: Join white in any corner, ch 3 for first dc, (2 dc, ch 2, 3 dc) in same corner, * (ch 2, popcorn in next ch-2 sp) 3 times, ch 2, (3 dc, ch 2, 3 dc) in corner, rep from * around, sl st to top of beg ch. Fasten off.

Rnd 5: Join blue in any corner, ch 3 for first dc, (2 dc, ch 2, 3 dc) in corner, * dc in each of next 3 dc, 2 dc in next ch-2 sp, (dc in next popcorn, dc in next ch-2 sp) twice, dc in next popcorn, 2 dc in next ch-2 sp **, dc in each of next 3 dc, (3 dc, ch 2, 3 dc) in corner, rep from * around, end last rep at **, sl st to top of beg ch. Fasten off.

WHIRLIGIG

COUNTRY TWEED

BLUE STAR

WHIRLIGIG

MATERIALS
Worsted-weight wool-blend: brown, blue.
Worsted-weight acrylic: off-white.
Size H crochet hook, or size to obtain gauge.

GAUGE
Square = 5″.

DIRECTIONS
With brown, ch 6, join with a sl st to form a ring.

Rnd 1: Ch 4 for first tr, 15 tr in ring, sl st to top of beg ch.

Rnd 2: Ch 6 for first tr and ch 2, * tr in next tr, ch 2, rep from * around, sl st to 4th ch of beg ch. Fasten off.

Rnd 3: Join blue in any tr, ch 3 for first dc, (2 dc, ch 1, 3 dc) in same st for corner, * (dc in next ch-2 sp, dc in next tr) 3 times, dc in next sp **, (3 dc, ch 1, 3 dc) in next tr for corner, rep from * around, end last rep at **, sl st to top of beg ch. Fasten off.

Rnd 4: Join off-white in any corner, ch 3 for first dc, (2 dc, ch 1, 3 dc) in same corner, * sk 2 dc, dc in each of next 9 dc, sk 2 dc, (3 dc, ch 1, 3 dc) in corner, rep from * around, sl st to top of beg ch. Fasten off.

BLUE STAR

MATERIALS
Worsted-weight acrylic: blue.
Size H crochet hook, or size to obtain gauge.

GAUGE
Square = 7″.

DIRECTIONS
Ch 6, join with a sl st to form a ring.

Rnd 1: Ch 4 for first tr, 2 tr in ring, ch 10, (3 tr in ring, ch 10) 3 times, sl st to top of beg ch.

Rnd 2: Ch 1, * sc in each of next 3 tr, (5 sc, 2 dc, 5 sc) in next lp, rep from * 3 times more, sl st to first sc.

Rnd 3: Sl st in next st, ch 10 for first dtr and ch 5, * dtr in same st, ch 5, sc bet sts of next 2-dc group, ch 5, sk 7 sc, dtr in next sc **, ch 5, rep from * around, end last rep at **, sl st to 5th ch of beg ch.

Rnd 4: Sl st in next sp, ch 4 for first tr, (2 tr, ch 3, 3 tr) in same sp, * (5 tr in next sp) twice **, (3 tr, ch 3, 3 tr) in next sp for corner, rep from * around, end last rep at **, sl st to top of beg ch.

Rnd 5: Ch 1, sc in same st, sc in each of next 2 tr, * 3 sc in corner sp, sc evenly to next corner, rep from * around, sl st to first sc. Fasten off.

COUNTRY TWEED

MATERIALS
Worsted-weight wool: variegated brown and blue (A), blue (B).
Size H crochet hook, or size to obtain gauge.

GAUGE
Square = 5½″.

DIRECTIONS
With A, ch 6, join with a sl st to form a ring.

Rnd 1: Ch 3 for first dc, 15 dc in ring, sl st to top of beg ch. Fasten off.

Rnd 2: Make a sl knot with B, yo and insert hook from in front and from right to left around post of any dc on prev rnd, yo and draw up a lp, (yo and through 2 lps on hook) twice (beg dc/raised front completed), yo and insert hook from in front and from right to left around same dc post, complete dc as usual (1 dc/rf completed), * ch 3, sk 1 dc, 2 dc/rf around next dc post, rep from * around, ch 3, sl st to top of beg ch. Fasten off. Turn.

Rnd 3 (wrong side): Join A in any ch-3 sp, ch 3 for first dc, (dc, ch 3, 2 dc) in same sp, 3 dc in next ch-3 sp, * (2 dc, ch 3, 2 dc) in next ch-3 sp for corner, 3 dc in next ch-3 sp, rep from * twice more, sl st to top of beg ch. Fasten off.

Rnd 4 (wrong side): Join B in any corner, ch 3 for first dc, (2 dc, ch 3, 3 dc) in same corner, * dc evenly to next corner, (3 dc, ch 3, 3 dc) in next corner, rep from * twice more, dc evenly to next corner, sl st to top of beg ch. Fasten off.

Rnd 5 (wrong side): Join A in any corner, ch 1, (2 sc, ch 1, 2 sc) in same corner, * sc evenly to next corner, (2 sc, ch 1, 2 sc) in corner, rep from * twice more, sc evenly to next corner, sl st to first sc. Fasten off.

WAGON WHEEL

MATERIALS

Sportweight cotton: brown, olive, beige.
Size F crochet hook, or size to obtain gauge.

GAUGE

Motif = 6″ diameter.

DIRECTIONS

With brown, ch 8, join with a sl st to form a ring.
Rnd 1: Ch 1, 12 sc in ring, sl st to first sc.

QUEEN ANNE'S LACE

SNOWFLAKE

WAGON WHEEL

Rnd 2: Ch 3 for first dc, dc in same st, (ch 5, sk 1 st, 2 dc in next st) 5 times, ch 5, sl st to top of beg ch. Fasten off.

Rnd 3: Join olive in any sp, ch 1, * (sc, 7 dc, sc) in ch-5 sp, rep from * 5 times more, sl st to first sc.

Rnd 4: Ch 1, sc bet next 2 sc, * ch 6, sk next 2 dc, dc in each of next 5 dc, ch 6, sc bet next 2 sc, ch 6 **, sc in same sp, rep from * around, end last rep at **, sl st to first sc. Fasten off.

Rnd 5: Join beige in lp just made, sc in same lp, * ch 3, sc in next lp, ch 4, sk 2 dc, sc in next dc, ch 4, sk 2 dc, sc in next lp, ch 3, sc in next lp, rep from * around, sl st to first sc.

Rnd 6: Sl st in next lp, sc in same lp, (ch 4, sc in next lp) 3 times, * ch 4, sc in next sc, (ch 4, sc in next lp) 4 times, rep from * 5 times more, ch 4, sc in next sc, ch 4, sl st to first sc. Fasten off.

Rnd 7: Join brown in any lp, ch 1, work 4 sc in each lp around, sl st to first sc. Fasten off.

SNOWFLAKE

MATERIALS
Sportweight cotton: light blue, gray.
Size F crochet hook, or size to obtain gauge.

GAUGE
Square = 4¼″.

DIRECTIONS
Note: Carry color not in use across row by working over it with the next group of sts. To avoid holes when changing colors, bring up new color from under dropped color. Always bring up new color as last yo of old color.

Square: With blue, ch 8, join with a sl st to form a ring.

Rnd 1: Ch 3 for first dc, 19 dc in ring, sl st to top of beg ch — 20 dc counting beg ch. Drop blue, but do not fasten off.

Rnd 2: Join gray and ch 3 for first dc, dc in next dc, * with blue and keeping last lp of each st on hook, work 4 dc in next st, yo with gray and through all lps on hook (cluster completed), with gray, dc in each of next 2 dc, ch 2 for corner, dc in each of next 2 dc, rep from * around, sl st to top of beg ch.

Rnd 3: With gray, ch 3 for first dc, dc in same sp, * dc in next dc, with blue, cluster in next dc, dc in next dc, cluster in next dc, with gray, dc in next dc **, (2 dc, ch 2, 2 dc) in corner, rep from * around, end last rep at **, 2 dc in beg corner, ch 2, sl st to top of beg ch.

Rnd 4: With gray, ch 3 for first dc, dc in same sp, * dc in each of next 4 sts, with blue, cluster in next dc, with gray, dc in each of next 4 sts **, (2 dc, ch 2, 2 dc) in corner, rep from * around, end last rep at **, 2 dc in beg corner, ch 2, sl st to top of beg ch. Fasten off blue.

Rnd 5: Ch 1, sc in same st, * sc evenly to next corner, (2 sc, ch 2, 2 sc) in corner, rep from * around, sl st to first sc. Fasten off.

QUEEN ANNE'S LACE

MATERIALS
Fingering-weight cotton: beige.
Size #7 steel crochet hook, or size to obtain gauge.

GAUGE
Motif = 6½″ diameter.

DIRECTIONS
Ch 10, join with a sl st to form a ring.

Rnd 1: Ch 3 for first dc, 23 dc in ring, sl st to top of beg ch.

Rnd 2: Ch 1, sc in same st, * ch 8, sk 2 dc, sc in next dc, rep from * around, sl st to first sc.

Rnd 3: Sl st to center of next ch-8 lp, sc in same st, * (ch 9, sc in same st) 3 times, ch 4, sc in center of next lp, rep from * around, sl st to first sc.

Rnd 4: Sl st to center of next ch-9 lp, sc in same st, * (ch 5, sc in next lp) twice, ch 1, sc in next lp, rep from * around, sl st to first sc.

Rnd 5: Sc in ch-1 sp just made, * (8 dc in next ch-5 lp) twice, sc in next ch-1 sp, rep from * around, sl st to first sc.

Rnd 6: Ch 11 for first tr and ch 7, * sk 8-dc group, sc in sp bet 8-dc groups, ch 7, tr in next sc, ch 7, rep from * around, sl st to 4th ch of beg ch.

Rnd 7: Ch 3 for first dc, * 7 dc in next sp, dc in next st, rep from * around, sl st to top of beg ch.

Rnd 8: Ch 8 for first dc and ch 5, sl st in 4th ch from hook to make a picot, ch 1, * sk 2 dc, dc in next dc, ch 5, sl st in 4th ch from hook to make a picot, ch 1, rep from * around, sl st to 3rd ch of beg ch. Fasten off.

CROSSED STITCHES

MATERIALS
Worsted-weight acrylic: burgundy, green.
Size E crochet hook, or size to obtain gauge.

GAUGE
Square = 5".

DIRECTIONS
With burgundy, ch 4, join with a sl st to form a ring.

Rnd 1 (wrong side): Ch 1, 8 sc in ring, sl st to bk lp of first sc. Turn.

Rnd 2 (right side): Ch 1, working in bk lps only, 3 sc in same st for corner, sc in next st, * 3 sc in next st for corner, sc in next st, rep from * twice more, sl st to bk lp of first sc. Turn.

Rnd 3: Working in bk lps only, * sc evenly to next corner, 3 sc in corner, rep from * around, sl st to first sc. Turn.

Rnds 4-7: Rep rnd 3. Fasten off after rnd 7.

Rnd 8: Join green in any corner, ch 5 for first dc and ch 2, dc in same st, * [sk 2 sts, dc in next st, ch 2, working behind first dc, dc in first sk st (cross dc completed)] 4 times, sk 1 st, dc in corner st, dc in sk st before corner, ch 2, sk first st of cross dc, dc in next st, ch 2, dc in last corner st (corner cross dc completed), rep from * around, sl st to 3rd ch of beg ch. Fasten off.

Rnd 9: Join burgundy in any corner, ch 3 for first dc, dc in same sp, * (2 dc in next sp) to next corner, (2 dc, ch 2, 2 dc) in corner, rep from * around, sl st to top of beg ch. Fasten off.

STRIPES

MATERIALS
Sportweight cotton slubbed texture: gray.
Bulky-weight wool: burgundy, green.
Size G crochet hook, or size to obtain gauge.

GAUGE
Rectangle = 8" x 7".

DIRECTIONS
Rectangle: With gray, ch 37.

Row 1: Dc in 3rd ch from hook and each ch across. Fasten off. Turn.

Row 2: Join burgundy, ch 1, sc in each st across. Fasten off. Turn.

Rows 3 and 4: Join gray, ch 3 for first dc, dc in each st across. Turn. Fasten off after row 4.

Row 5: Join burgundy, ch 1, sc in each st across. Fasten off. Turn.

Rows 6-8: Join gray, ch 3 for first dc, dc in each st across. Turn. Fasten off after row 8.

Row 9: Join green, ch 1, sc in each st across. Fasten off. Turn.

Rows 10-16: Join gray, ch 3 for first dc, dc in each st across. Turn. Fasten off after row 16.

Border: Join gray with sl st in any corner, * 3 sc in corner, sc evenly to next corner, rep from * around. Fasten off.

Finishing: With right side facing and burgundy, insert hook in sp bet 4th and 5th sts from left-hand edge at bottom of first row and draw up a lp. * Insert hook in sp bet sts in row directly above, yo and draw through lp on hook, rep from * to top edge of square to make a vertical stripe. *Note:* Work surface sts fairly loosely so that piece will lie flat. To work additional rows: Sk 3 sts to the right and work a row with green, sk 3 more sts to the right and work a row with burgundy.

CROSSED STITCHES

STRIPES

CHRISTMAS PICOTS

CHRISTMAS BOWS

CHRISTMAS PICOTS

MATERIALS

Worsted-weight acrylic: green, red.
Size H crochet hook, or size to obtain gauge.

GAUGE

Square = 5¼″.

DIRECTIONS

With green, ch 3, join with a sl st to form a ring.

Rnd 1: Ch 1, 8 sc in ring, sl st to first sc. Ch 1, turn.

Rnd 2: Working in bk lps only, sc in same st, sc in next st, * 3 sc in next st for corner, sc in next st, rep from * twice more, 2 sc in same st as first sc, sl st to first sc. Ch 1, turn.

Rnd 3: Working in bk lps only, * sc in each sc to next corner, 3 sc in center sc of corner, rep from * around, end with 2 sc in same st as first sc, sl st to first sc. Ch 1, turn.

Rnds 4-7: Rep rnd 3. Fasten off after rnd 7.

Rnd 8: Join red in center sc of any corner, sc in same st, * ch 3, sl st in 3rd ch from hook to make a picot, sk 1 sc, sc in next sc, rep from * around, sl st to first sc. Fasten off.

CHRISTMAS BOWS

MATERIALS

Worsted-weight brushed acrylic-nylon blend: green, red.
Size F crochet hook, or size to obtain gauge.

GAUGE

Square = 4″.

DIRECTIONS

Square: With green, ch 6, join with a sl st to form a ring.

Rnd 1: Ch 4 for first tr, dc, tr, * ch 2 for corner, tr, dc, tr, rep from * twice more, ch 2 for corner, sl st to top of beg ch.

Rnd 2: Ch 3 for first dc, dc in each of next 2 sts, * (dc, tr, ch 2, tr, dc) in next ch-2 sp for corner, dc in each of next 3 sts, rep from * around, sl st to top of beg ch.

Rnd 3: Ch 3 for first dc, * dc evenly to next corner, (dc, tr, ch 2, tr, dc) in corner, rep from * around, sl st to top of beg ch.

Rnd 4: Ch 3 for first dc, * dc evenly to next corner, (dc, tr, ch 2, tr, dc) in corner, rep from * around, sl st to top of beg ch. Fasten off.

Bow (make 2): With red, ch 31, sc in 2nd ch from hook and each ch across. Fasten off. Tie in a bow. Tack bow to square at bottom of 8th st of rnd 4 (see photograph). Rep for other bow.

LACED WITH RIBBON

STARBURST

LACED WITH RIBBON

MATERIALS
Sportweight wool: green.
Size H crochet hook, or size to obtain gauge.
15" (⅛"-wide) ribbon.

GAUGE
Square = 3½".

DIRECTIONS
Square: Ch 4, join with a sl st to form a ring.
    Rnd 1: Ch 1, 8 sc in ring, sl st to first sc.
    Rnd 2: Ch 1, 2 sc in same st, 2 sc in each sc around, sl st to first sc.
    Rnd 3: Ch 1, 2 sc in same st, * sc in next sc, 2 sc in next sc, rep from * around, sl st to bk lp of first sc — 24 sc.
    Rnd 4: Ch 1, working in bk lps only, sc in each sc around, sl st to first sc.
    Rnd 5: Ch 5 for first dc and ch 2, dc in same st, * sk 1 sc, (dc, ch 2, dc) in next sc, rep from * around, sl st to 3rd ch of beg ch.
    Rnd 6: Ch 1, sc in same st, sc in next ch-2 sp, * hdc in next st, dc in next st, 3 tr in next ch-2 sp, dc in next st, hdc in next st, sc in next ch-2 sp, sc in each of next 2 sts, sc in next ch-2 sp, rep from * around, sl st to first sc. Fasten off.

Finishing: With right side of square facing, weave ribbon through sts of rnd 4 and tie in a bow.

STARBURST

MATERIALS
Worsted-weight acrylic-mohair blend: blue, pink, green, black.
Size E crochet hook, or size to obtain gauge.

GAUGE
Square = 5".

DIRECTIONS
With blue, ch 6, join with a sl st to form a ring.
    Rnd 1: (Sc in ring, ch 4, 2 tr in ring, ch 4) 4 times, sl st to first sc. Fasten off.
    Rnd 2: Join pink in any sc, ch 11 for first tr and ch 7, * sc bet 2 tr, ch 7, tr in next sc, ch 7, rep from * around, sl st to 4th ch of beg ch. Fasten off.
    Rnd 3: Join green in any tr, ch 4 for first tr, 2 tr in same st, * ch 1, sc in next ch-7 lp, ch 1, (2 tr, ch 2, 2 tr) in next sc for corner, ch 1, sc in next ch-7 lp, ch 1 **, 3 tr in next tr, rep from * around, end last rep at **, sl st to top of beg ch. Fasten off.
    Rnd 4: Join black in bk lp of tr after any ch-2 corner sp, * working in bk lps only, sc evenly to next corner sp, sc in bk lp of first ch, ch 1, sc in bk lp of next ch, rep from * around, sl st to first sc. Fasten off.

Yarn Information

The following is a complete list of the yarns used for each project pictured in the book. Contact your local yarn or craft shop to obtain the yarn shown. If you are unable to locate the yarn in your area, or for further information, write the yarn company at the address listed under Yarn Sources below.

■ ■ ■

CHAPTER 1
Elegant Afghans

Ivy League Afghan, page 14: Aarlan, Swa Laine, 25 skeins Multicolor Heather (Blue, Green, and Red) #M2, 12 skeins each Green #G1, Red #R1, Blue #B1, 15 skeins Multicolor Heather (Navy and Red) #M1.

Evening News, page 15: Classic Elite Yarns, Cambridge, 9 skeins Medium Gray #3923; La Gran, 7 skeins Light Pearl Gray #6503. Andean Yarns, Alpaquita SuperFina, 8 skeins Dark Oxford Gray #43. Scheepjeswol, Superwash Wool, 6 skeins Medium Gray #2906. Kiwi Imports, Perendale, 10 skeins Dark Oxford Gray #402, 8 skeins Pearl Gray #403. Pingouin, Escapade, 2 skeins Gray Heather #13.

Bouquet of Primroses, page 18: Scotts Woolen Mill, Dynasty, 15 skeins Mauve, 12 skeins Rose.

Field of Pansies, page 20: DMC Corporation, Perle Cotton Size 5, 5 skeins Yellow #307, 3 skeins Medium Purple #208, 5 skeins Deep Purple #550, 4 balls Rust #902, 3 skeins Medium Rust #355, 75 skeins Green #319.

Cascade of Roses, page 22: Coats & Clark, Size 10, 10 balls Ecru.

A Classic Coverlet, page 24: Coats & Clark, Knit CroSheen, 53 balls Ecru.

Gingerbread Throw, page 27: Berroco, Dante, 16 skeins Multicolor Brown, Blue, Beige, and Lavender #1129, 4 skeins Multicolor Beige, Off-white, Tan, Light Blue, and Brown #1093. William Unger & Co., Riccione, 6 skeins Light Brown #320.

Soft Pinks, page 28: Brunswick Yarns, Moonbeams, 9 balls Willow #8520, 10 balls Pale Peach #8507, 8 balls Khaki #8509.

Crocheted Sampler, page 30: Reynolds Yarns, Clover, 6 skeins Green #28, 9 skeins Cream #58. Lily Craft Products, Sugar 'n Cream Cotton Mousse, 7 skeins Green #17. Tahki Yarns, Cotton Twist, 6 skeins Apricot #912A. Berger du Nord, Linen/Cotton, 7 skeins Cream #8402. Classic Elite Yarns, Applause, 7 skeins Pastel Blend #1801.

Pastel Hearts, page 34: William Unger & Co., Plantation, 1 skein each Pink #307, Apricot #324, Light Yellow #117, Light Green #548, Light Blue #207, Lavender #665; Roly Sport, 10 skeins white.

Cozy Colors, page 36: Brunswick Yarns, Windrush, skeins in the following amounts: 1 Juniper #90571, 1 Medium Juniper #90572, 1 Dark Juniper #90573, 1 Dark Jade #90593, 2 Medium Jade #90592, 2 Jade #90591, 2 Light Aqua #90390, 3 Aqua #90391, 3 Medium Aqua #90392, 3 Light Blue #9002, 3 Light Blue Velvet #90813, 3 Medium Blue Velvet #90812, 3 Light Powder Blue #90111, 3 Medium Country Blue #90762, 3 Dark Country Blue #90763, 2 Light Hyacinth #90161, 2 Hyacinth #90162, 2 Dark Hyacinth #90163, 1 Damson #90023, 1 Mulberry #90024, 1 Sugar Plum #90025, 1 Light Sugar Plum #90030.

Granny's Favorites, page 38: Brunswick Yarns, Pearl, 13 balls Lavender #5904, 4 skeins each Dusty Pink #5922, Smoke Blue #5921, Orchid #5916, 1 skein Silver Gray #5915.

Blanket of Lavender, page 40: Berger du Nord, Linen/Cotton, 7 skeins Blue #8396, 13 skeins Purple #8398.

Mosaic Squares, page 42: Rowan Yarns, Designer Collection 4-ply Cabled Mercerized Cotton, 1 cone each Dark Green #329, Beige #325, Light Green #327, Light Gray #316, Medium Gray #317, Dark Gray #318, Lavender #311.

Country Squares, page 44: Tahki Yarns, Cotton Twist, 11 skeins each Taupe #778, Beige #264.

Shades of the Southwest, page 46: Copley USA, Popcorn, 8 skeins White/Orange #824. William Unger & Co., Fluffy, 5 skeins Light Orange #582, 3 skeins Medium Orange #584, 3 skeins Dark Orange #497.

CHAPTER 2
Lacy Linens

Mother's Finest, page 50: Coats & Clark, Knit CroSheen, 10 balls Cream.

Dresden Kitchen, page 51: Large square: Reynolds Yarns, Saucy, 2 skeins each White #800, Light Blue #232, Medium Dark Blue #292. Small square: DMC Corporation, Cebelia Size 10, 1 skein each White, Light Blue #800, Medium Dark Blue #798.

Basket Liner, page 54: Coats & Clark, Size 30, 6 balls White, 4 balls Shaded Yellows #19, 2 balls Shaded Greens #21.

Flower Coasters, page 56: DMC Corporation, Cebelia Size 30, 1 ball White.

Old English Blocks, page 58: DMC Corporation, Cordonnet Size 20, 6 balls Ecru.

Trousseau Treasure, page 60: DMC Corporation, Cebelia Size 30, 1 ball Ecru.

Pretty & Pink, page 62: Coats & Clark, Size 30, 1 ball Shaded Pinks #15, 2 balls White.

Blossoms, page 64: Brunswick Yarns, Windmist, 9 skeins Peach Ice #2822, 8 skeins Soft Pastel Ombre #2895. William Unger & Co., Fluffy, 3 skeins Aqua #583.

Homespun Web, page 66: DMC Corporation, Cebelia Size 30, 1 ball Ecru.

Loop d'Linen, page 67: Coats & Clark, Size 50, 1 ball White; Size 30, 10 yards White.

CHAPTER 3
Glorious Gifts

CHAPTER 4
Christmas Crochet

CHAPTER 5
Pattern Portfolio

Butterfly, page 132: Reynolds Yarns, Saucy, White.

Popcorn Granny, page 132: Aarlan, Cottonella, Blue #C6146. Brunswick Yarns, Alaska, White.

Whirligig, page 134: Caron International, Glencannon, Soft Brown #1108, Blue Gray #807. Coats & Clark, Red Heart, Off-white.

Blue Star, page 134: Coats & Clark, Red Heart, Blue Gray #807.

Country Tweed, page 134: Tahki Yarns, Donegal Tweed, Multicolor Brown and Blue #896. Filatura Di Crosa, Sympathie, Blue #914.

Wagon Wheel, page 136: Aarlan, Cottonella, Brown #6103, Olive #6146; Fleurette, Beige #4490.

Snowflake, page 136: Aarlan, Fleurette, Light Blue #C4474, Gray Beige #C4490.

Queen Anne's Lace, page 136: Rowan Yarns, Designer Collection 4-ply Cabled Mercerized Cotton, Mushroom #325.

Crossed Stitches, page 138: Brunswick Yarns, Pearl, Burgundy #5924, Forest Green #5925.

Stripes, page 138: Lily Craft Products, Sugar 'n Cream Cotton Mousse, Light Gray #313. Aarlan, Swa Laine, Burgundy #R2, Dark Green #G1.

Christmas Picots, page 140: Coats & Clark, Red Heart, Paddy Green #686, Red Cardinal #911.

Christmas Bows, page 140: Brunswick Yarns, Alaska, Chinese Red #9206, Emerald Green #9207.

Laced with Ribbon, page 141: Filatura Di Crosa, Stella, Forest Green #432.

Starburst, page 141: Aarlan, Charmeuse, Blue #4977, Hot Pink #4971, Green #4976, Black #4967.

YARN SOURCES

Aarlan
21 Adley Road
Cambridge, MA 02158

Andean Yarns
no address available

Berger du Nord
c/o Bernat Yarn & Craft
Depot and Mendon Streets
Uxbridge, MA 01569

Bernat Yarn & Craft Corp.
Depot and Mendon Streets
Uxbridge, MA 01569

Berroco, Inc.
Elmdale Road
P.O. Box 367
Uxbridge, MA 01569

Brunswick Yarns
P.O. Box 276
Pickens, SC 29671

Bucilla
230 Fifth Avenue
New York, NY 10001

Caron International
P.O. Box 300
Rochelle, IL 61068

Classic Elite Yarns
12 Perkins Street
Lowell, MA 01854

Coats & Clark, Inc.
P.O. Box 1010, Dept. CS
Toccoa, GA 30577

Copley USA, Inc.
383 Main Avenue
Norwalk, CT 06851

Darlaine Yarn Co.
P.O. Box 300
Highway 45
Jamestown, SC 29453

DMC Corporation
107 Trumbull Street
Elizabeth, NJ 07206

Filatura Di Crosa
c/o Stacy Charles Collection
117 Dobbins Street
Brooklyn, NY 11222

Georges Picaud
c/o Merino Wool Co., Inc.
16 West 19th Street
New York, NY 10011

Hayfield of London
c/o Cascade Yarns
204 Third Avenue South
Seattle, WA 98104

Kiwi Imports, Inc.
no address available

Lily Craft Products
c/o B. Blumenthal & Co.
140 Kero Road
Carlstadt, NJ 07072

Madeira USA, Inc.
56 Primrose Drive
Oshea Industrial Park
Laconia, NH 03246

Natura
c/o National Yarn Crafts
183 Madison Avenue
New York, NY 10016

Phildar
6110 Northbelt Highway
Atlanta, GA 30071

Pingouin Yarn
P.O. Box 100
Highway 45
Jamestown, SC 29453

Reynolds Yarns, Inc.
15 Oser Avenue
Hauppauge, NY 11788

Rowan Yarns
c/o Westminster Trading
5 North Boulevard
Amherst, NH 03031

Scheepjeswol USA, Inc.
c/o Juniper Yarns
199 Trade Zone Drive
Ronkonkoma, NY 11779

Scotts Woolen Mill, Inc.
528 Jefferson Avenue
Bristol, PA 19007

Swedish Yarn Imports
P.O. Box 2112
Jamestown, NC 27282

Tahki Imports, Inc.
11 Graphic Place
Moonachie, NJ 07074

William Unger & Co.
230 Fifth Avenue
New York, NY 10001